INTEGRITY SYSTEMS FOR OCCUPATIONS

AF763682

Law, Ethics and Governance Series

Series Editor: Charles Sampford, Director, Key Centre for Ethics, Law, Justice and Governance, Griffith University, Australia

Recent history has emphasised the potentially devastating effects of governance failures in governments, government agencies, corporations and the institutions of civil society. 'Good governance' is seen as necessary, if not crucial, for economic success and human development. Although the disciplines of law, ethics, politics, economics and management theory can provide insights into the governance of organisations, governance issues can only be dealt with by interdisciplinary studies, combining several (and sometimes all) of those disciplines. This series aims to provide such interdisciplinary studies for students, researchers and relevant practitioners.

Recent titles in the series

Promoting Integrity
Evaluating and Improving Public Institutions
Edited by Brian W. Head, A.J. Brown and Carmel Connors
ISBN 978-0-7546-4986-1

Protracted Displacement in Asia
No Place to Call Home
Edited by Howard Adelman
ISBN 978-0-7546-7238-8

Governing the Heroin Trade
From Treaties to Treatment
Melissa Bull
ISBN 978-0-7546-7121-3

Islam Beyond Conflict
Indonesian Islam and Western Political Theory
Edited by Azyumardi Azra and Wayne Hudson
ISBN 978-0-7546-7092-6

Re-envisioning Sovereignty
The End of Westphalia?
Edited by Trudy Jacobsen, Charles Sampford and Ramesh Thakur
ISBN 978-0-7546-7260-9

Integrity Systems for Occupations

ANDREW ALEXANDRA
University of Melbourne, Australia
SEUMAS MILLER
Charles Sturt University, Australia,
The Australian National University, Australia
and Delft University of Technology, the Netherlands

Routledge
Taylor & Francis Group
LONDON AND NEW YORK

First published 2010 by Ashgate Publishing

Published 2016 by Routledge
2 Park Square, Milton Park, Abingdon, Oxfordshire OX14 4RN
711 Third Avenue, New York, NY 10017, USA

First issued in paperback 2016

Routledge is an imprint of the Taylor & Francis Group, an informa business

Copyright © 2010 Andrew Alexandra and Seumas Miller

Andrew Alexandra and Seumas Miller have asserted their right under the Copyright, Designs and Patents Act, 1988, to be identified as the authors of this work.

All rights reserved. No part of this book may be reprinted or reproduced or utilised in any form or by any electronic, mechanical, or other means, now known or hereafter invented, including photocopying and recording, or in any information storage or retrieval system, without permission in writing from the publishers.

Notice:
Product or corporate names may be trademarks or registered trademarks, and are used only for identification and explanation without intent to infringe.

British Library Cataloguing in Publication Data
Alexandra, Andrew, 1951-
Integrity systems for occupations. -- (Law, ethics and governance series)
1. Professional ethics. 2. Labor discipline.
I. Title II. Series III. Miller, Seumas.
174-dc22

Library of Congress Cataloging-in-Publication Data
Alexandra, Andrew, 1951-
Integrity systems for occupations / by Andrew Alexandra and Seumas Miller.
p. cm. -- (Law, ethics, and governance)
Includes bibliographical references and indexes.
ISBN 978-0-7546-7749-9 (hardback)
1. Organizational behavior. 2. Professional ethics. I. Miller, Seumas. II. Title.

HD58.7.A434 2009
174--dc22

2009032354

ISBN 13: 978-1-138-27692-5 (pbk)
ISBN 13: 978-0-7546-7749-9 (hbk)

Contents

Acknowledgements

The contents of this book reflect, and draw from, work we have done over a period of years. Our thinking about occupational integrity systems benefited considerably from working on two reports for professional bodies. These were: Andrew Alexandra, Seumas Miller, Tom Campbell, Dean Cocking and Kevin White, *Professionalisation, Ethics and Integrity: The Promotion of Professional Ethical Standards and the Protection of Clients and Customers*, Report for the Professional Standards Council, 2006; and Seumas Miller and Mathew Ward, *Complaints and Self-Assessment Data Analysis in Relation to Incorporated Legal Practices*, Report for the Office of the Legal Services Commissioner, 2006.

We owe thanks to our fellow authors, and to Bernie Marden, and Rob Lawson (of the Professional Standards Council), as well as Steve Mark and Molly Hutcherson (of the Office of the Legal Services Commissioner) for their support. Here we should also thank Charles Sampford, the editor of the series in which this volume appears, for his guidance and encouragement, and Ned Dobos for his work in preparing the book for publication.

Thanks also go to the relevant editors and publishers in relation to the following publications from which material in this book has been taken. Andrew Alexandra and Seumas Miller 'Needs, Moral Self-consciousness and Professional Roles', *Professional Ethics,* vol. 5, nos.1 & 2, 1996; 'Ethical Theory, "Common Morality" and Professional Obligations', *Theoretical Medicine and Bioethics*, vol. 30, no. 1, 2009; *Ethics in Practice: Moral Theory and the Professions*, Sydney: University of NSW Press, 2009. Seumas Miller, *Social Action: A Teleological Account*, New York: Cambridge University Press, 2001; *Model Code of Ethics,* Sydney: Professional Standards Council, 2002; 'Corruption', *Stanford Encylopedia of Philosophy*, Summer edition, 2005; 'Institutions, Integrity Systems and Market Actors', in Justin O'Brien (ed.), *Private Equity, Corporate Governance and the Dynamics of Capital Market Regulation*, London: Imperial College of London Press, 2007; 'Research in Applied Ethics: Problems and Perspectives', *Philosophia*, vol. 37, no. 2, 2009; *The Moral Foundations of Social Institutions: A Philosophical Study*, New York: Cambridge University Press, 2009. Seumas Miller, Peter Roberts and Edward Spence, *Corruption and Anti-Corruption*, Saddle River, NJ: Prentice Hall, 2005.

Introduction

Ethics

Ethics or morality is about what actions an individual person or member of an occupation ought to do, and it is about what kind of character an individual person or member of an occupation ought to have. It is also about what features the organizations that employ members of specific occupations ought to have.

Although ethics is concerned with what ought to be done, or not done, it does not embrace the entire sphere of prescribed or proscribed actions, for there are 'oughts' other than the ethical or moral 'oughts'. Sometimes we say things like, 'You ought to have said "Hello" to Jack'. Here, the 'ought' is one of etiquette. You ought to, because it is rude not to greet people; rude, but not necessarily unethical or immoral.

We also need to distinguish ethics or morality from aesthetics. Sometimes we say that that painting is good, or that so and so ought not to wear green trousers with a blue shirt, or shocking-pink suits. Here, we have in mind aesthetics; it is not unethical or immoral to dress in these ways.

The terms 'ethics' and 'morality' are often used interchangeably. However, sometimes ethics is distinguished from morality. One way of making the distinction is as follows. Morality is about minimum standards of behaviour and attitude. Do not kill the innocent; do not tell lies; do not steal; do not commit fraud. These are all minimum standards of behaviour; they are moral principles. On the other hand – in this way of thinking – ethics is a wider notion. Ethics involves ideals and aspirations; it goes beyond minimum standards. A doctor who is competent, and is not negligent, might not be engaged in immoral behaviour. Nevertheless, such a doctor might not be a good doctor. To be a good doctor implies doing more than merely complying with minimum standards. For example, a good doctor would have a caring attitude to his or her patients.

Henceforth, we will distinguish ethics and morality in this above-described way. Morality therefore refers to minimum standards, whiles ethics refers to a wider field of value that embraces notions of what is good and worth aspiring to – ideals as well as minimum standards.

Let us now turn to a general account or map of the ethical or moral terrain. In thinking and reasoning about moral or ethical questions there are a number of key concepts and distinctions. We will now introduce some of the more important of these.

First, we need to distinguish between actions, habits and attitudes. Actions are morally right or morally wrong or neither. Examples of actions normally regarded as morally right are truth-telling, paying one's debts and providing for one's children. Examples of actions normally regarded as morally wrong are breaking a promise, killing an innocent person, and thieving. Examples of actions that are normally regarded as neither morally right nor morally wrong are going for a walk, drinking a bottle of lemonade or buying the Sunday papers.

If we now turn to ethical actions, as opposed to merely morally acceptable actions, then we can see that they tend to be actions in conformity with ideals or aspirations. For example, engaging in unpaid voluntary work for charitable organizations, or not taking advantage of one's competitor when – owing to bad luck – they are in an unfortunate situation.

Notwithstanding the distinction between minimum standards and ideals, the boundary between these points is blurred: there is a considerable grey area. Moreover, it is important to note that attending only to minimum standards – being a 'rule addict' and eschewing ideals – is an ultimately unsustainable position. Rule addicts will tend to lose sight of the values, including the ideals, that inform even the rules embodying minimum standards; ultimately this is corrosive of conformity to minimum standards, as well as the realization of ideals.

Habits are dispositions to action that are typically performed by a person. For example, Winston Churchill had the habit of smoking cigars. Habits include virtues, such as courage, honesty and determination, as well as vices, such as cowardice, corruption and dishonesty. Winston Churchill was said to be a courageous leader because he frequently or habitually made hard decisions in the service of his country. In the 1990s, the New South Wales police officer Chook Fowler was said to be corrupt because he consistently or habitually engaged in illegal activity to enrich himself. Some habits are neither virtues nor vices. For example, the habit of taking the dog for a walk in the early morning would not normally be regarded as either a virtue or a vice.

Once again, vices tend to call for moral condemnation; people who are corrupt or dishonest fail to meet minimum standards. On the other hand, persons possessed of virtues tend to be seen as ethical; they have dispositions to do what is good. They do more than merely avoid wrongdoing. However, once again there is a grey area here between minimum standards and ideals.

As noted above, the key property of virtues and vices is that they are elements of character; they are to do with what a person is, as opposed to what a person might do on some particular occasion. Clearly character, and thus virtues and vices, are of central importance in ethics.

Affective attitudes, including feelings and emotions, are not actions as such; nor are they habits or merely dispositions to act. A person can obey all the rules, even do so as a matter of habit, and yet have a 'bad attitude'.

As with actions and habits, affective attitudes can be classified into those that are by and large good, such as a caring or sympathetic or sensitive attitude, and those that are for the most part morally wrong, such as an attitude of hatred or contempt. Naturally, some attitudes would not normally be regarded as either good or morally wrong, e.g. the attitude or feeling of excitement generated at the thought of being paid a large salary. Moreover, there is a grey area here between morally problematic attitudes, such as hatred, and attitudes that one ought ideally to have, but ought not to suffer moral condemnation if one did not experience them, e.g. friendliness.

Virtues and Character

Moral principles give us rules by which to act. This has its advantages, since rules are things that can be made explicit and apply equally to everybody. But those theorists who have insisted on the importance of virtues and, more generally, of character, have pointed out that given the range of situations we find ourselves in and the complexities of the individuals we deal with, there often is no rule that can be meaningfully applied. In these cases we need what might be called moral judgement, and this is not something that can be reduced to a matter of rules or calculation.[1]

It is difficult, if not impossible, to come up with more than very general prescriptions for virtuous action for two reasons. First, the range, complexity and continually changing nature of the sorts of situations where we may have to act morally mean that we will never be able to come up with comprehensive action-guiding rules.

The second reason is connected to the first, but instead of focusing on the difference in particular circumstances, it looks to the difference in morally legitimate responses made by individuals to those circumstances. Different responses from different individuals might be morally appropriate in the very same circumstances, e.g. a child might be admonished by his parents but indulged by his grandparents in relation to some minor act of wrongdoing.

The possession and exercise of virtues (and vices) is partially constitutive of our character, they help make us the kind of person we are. But just as circumstances display an inexhaustible variety, so do people. Two good people can differ in which virtues they place more emphasis on, which they are more likely to manifest, and hence on their responses to particular situations. Although their responses may be different, they might both be seen as reasonable, even commendable.

The discussion of virtue as central to the moral realm harks back at least to Aristotle, writing almost two and half thousand years ago. Modern theorists of virtue still have to take Aristotle's views seriously.[2]

So far we have operated with an unanalysed notion of virtue and vice, assuming that courage, for example, is a virtue, in itself admirable, and cruelty a vice, to be despised.

1 See Alexandra A., and Miller, S. *Ethics in Practice: Moral Theory and the Professions*, Sydney: University of NSW Press, 2009, Chapter 4.

2 See Aristotle's *The Nichomachean Ethics* (any edition).

As Aristotle pointed out, the term 'virtue' has a range of uses, not all which bear moral implications. We can talk about the virtues of a knife, for instance – these include sharpness and ease of handling. We can similarly speak about the virtues of a clock, such as accuracy and quietness. Given that sharpness counts as a virtue in a knife, but not in a clock, what do these features of things have in common, such that they all can be called virtues? Each of them counts as a virtue because each helps the object in which they are found achieve its function. The function of a knife is to cut – being sharp allows the knife to cut, so sharpness is a virtue in a knife. The function of a clock is to keep time – accuracy is necessary for it to be able to keep time, so accuracy is a virtue in a clock. Another way of talking about functions in this sense is to speak of ends – the end for which a knife is intended is cutting and so on. We are now in a position to offer a general characterization of virtue. A virtue can be characterized as some property, the possession of which helps a thing achieve its end.

Such a characterization of virtue may look quite unexceptionable when applied to artefacts that have very clear functions. But what about human beings? First, let us tentatively adjust the characterization to fit more closely the notion of virtue as it applies to humans. A human virtue is some relatively stable aspect of someone's character, which disposes the person to act in a way that will help them achieve their end. This characterization begs the question: can it be said that *we* have ends? Well, sometimes at least we clearly do, when we occupy certain roles. The function of a doctor is to cure the sick, the function of a comedian is to make people laugh and so on. It is usually relatively simple to decide what are the various role virtues: courage in a soldier, diagnostic skill in a doctor, and so on – the qualities that help role holders achieve the ends of their role. We will look at these issues in more detail in Chapter 1. However, although it may be clear enough what the ends of people in their various occupational roles are supposed to be, and hence what the relevant occupational virtues are, it seems much harder to determine what the ends of human beings simply qua human beings are; or indeed if they have any ultimate end at all. Aristotle thought that just as is there a final end, a highest good, of say medicine, which provided the standard for judging a doctor's work, so there is a final end that we possess as people, and against which we can judge human behaviour and institutions.

Aristotle was quick to acknowledge that there is a whole variety of particular goods at which people actually aim – money, honour, friendship and so on – and which seem to have virtually nothing in common. Nevertheless, we can set up a kind of hierarchy amongst these goods. We can understand the place of a human or social good in this hierarchy in terms of means and ends. At the bottom of the hierarchy are those things that we value *only* as a means to some other end. So money is a good of this kind, since it has no intrinsic worth, it is valuable only in that it allows us to get other things that we value. (Some people – misers – do value money for its own sake, but they are simply making a mistake.) Next in the hierarchy come the things that we value not simply as means to ends, but also as ends in themselves, such as friendship, honour and pleasure. However, even these goods, although ends in themselves, are at the same time means to a further, and in Aristotle's view, final end. This end, at the top of the hierarchy, he calls *eudaimonia*. There is no exact equivalent for this term in English. It is often translated as 'happiness', but probably 'flourishing' is closer to Aristotle's meaning. This is the only good that is purely an end in itself. It is in the light of this good that we can assess aspects of our characters to decide if they are virtues or not. Do they, could they, help us flourish? If they do, they will count as virtues, if they don't they won't.

By itself, being told that those aspects of our character that help us flourish count as virtues is not going to help us much, until we know what constitutes flourishing. Aristotle's own answer to this question identifies flourishing strongly with the development and exercise of reason, which he takes to be the defining human property. We can, however, work with a less restrictive notion of flourishing. It is true that there is some controversy about whether certain kinds of lifestyles and behaviours count as flourishing or not. While some people think of the life of silence of Trappist monks as a kind of spiritual mutilation, others think of it as offering sublime rewards. But at the same time it is often very clear if someone's life can be thought of as flourishing. Someone who lives in pleasant surroundings, enjoying the company of congenial friends, doing interesting work, surely counts as having a flourishing life; and someone who lives in poverty and loneliness in a dangerous slum, does not have a flourishing life.

Moral Reasoning

As already in effect noted, morality or ethics is *practical*; it concerns what a person or group *ought to do*, and what a person or group *ought to be*. It comprises answers to questions such as: ought I buy a new car or spend the money on my son's education? Ought I to inform the police that my friend takes illegal drugs? Ought Jane to leave her husband? Ought I inform on a corrupt colleague? Ought I charge this impoverished client a smaller fee? What ought we to do? Should we turn away refugees from Afghanistan? Should we introduce voluntary euthanasia? Should the market fully determine the structure of fees paid to professionals?

Moral or ethical decision-making is, or ought to be, based on reasons, e.g. Jane ought to leave her husband because (for the reason) he is beating her up. Fees ought to be paid because (for the reason) clients promised to pay them.

Moreover, often there are reasons for and against a particular course of action, and therefore a *complex structure of reasons* is involved.[3] For example, in relation to insisting that one's client pay the full fee, there is at least one reason in favour of this; namely, the client in effect agreed to pay the set fee by virtue of knowing what the fee was and accepting the service. But there is also at least one reason against

---

3 See Alexandra, A., and Miller, S. *Ethics in Practice: Moral Theory and the Professions*, Sydney: University of NSW Press, 2009, Chapter 5.

insisting on the full fee, namely, the client is impoverished and cannot afford to pay it without suffering severe hardship as a result.

This complex structure of reasons or arguments involves *factual* claims, e.g. the fee is $*X*, the client's income is $*Y*, the service performed was the extraction of an extremely painful tooth. But it also involves ethical or *moral values* or moral normative claims, e.g. 'To suffer ongoing extreme pain is bad', 'A practitioner has a moral right to be paid a reasonable fee for services rendered'.

One pervasive form of reasoning in relation to both ethical and non-ethical issues is *means/end reasoning*, e.g. business people ought to reduce costs because this will lead to lower prices and increased profits. Moreover, much of the reasoning in ethics is means/end reasoning, e.g. a social worker ought to authorize this child to be taken from her family because the father is a child abuser and if the child is not removed then the child will suffer grave harm. Here the end – to protect the innocent child – is a moral end.

In ethical decision-making there is another form of reasoning, which we will refer to as *reasoning from moral or ethical principles*.

In relation to reasoning, there is a more general distinction to be made between so-called *theoretical reasoning*, and *practical reasoning*. Theoretical reasoning is reasoning about what is the case, about what is true. The aim of theoretical reasoning is to produce true beliefs. Practical reasoning is reasoning about what we ought to *do*. The aim of practical reasoning is to guide us to rational action; so means/end reasoning and reasoning from ethical principles are species of practical reasoning. We typically act in order to achieve outcomes that we take to be valuable. A practically rational action, then, will be one that produces the greatest, or at least sufficient, value. There is, of course, a variety of different kinds of value, including moral value as well as prudential value, financial value, aesthetic value and so on.

Although theoretical and practical reasoning are importantly different from each other, they are also intimately connected. In particular, when we are trying to decide what to do we usually have to draw on the results of theoretical reasoning. We must discover what courses of action are available to us, and we must work out what the likely consequences of those various possible actions are, and these are both matters of fact. In other words, we are only likely to be able to act rationally if we have true beliefs.

Both theoretical and practical reasoning can be seen as involving a two-step process. First, we should work out the considerations relevant to the issue at hand. Then we should decide what to believe (in the case of theoretical reasoning) or what to do (in the case of practical reasoning) on the basis of these considerations. The form of such a process is made explicit in the production of arguments in the sense of a certain kind of structure of sentences. In philosophical terminology, the considerations that are supposed to be relevant to the matter at hand are put in sentences called 'premises', while the sentences that represent the decisions we make on the basis of those considerations are referred to as 'conclusions'.

Consider the following simple example of an argument (a piece of reasoning from a moral principle).

Premise 1: I believe that lying is wrong (moral principle).
Premise 2: Telling this suspected fraudster that I will not report him is a lie.
Conclusion: I ought not to tell this suspect that I will not report him.

This argument is not a *deductive* argument since the conclusion could be false even though the premises were true, e.g. if I am an auditor and telling the suspect the truth would enable him to flee the country and escape. Nor is the argument *inductive*, since a moral principle is a normative claim, not an inductive generalization; nor is it necessarily based on induction. Further, the argument is not a piece of means/end reasoning since there are no goals or desires in the premises.

Where there are competing moral reasons, e.g. telling a lie versus preventing a fraudster to escape, then a balance has to be struck on the basis of reasons.

Reflecting the two-step process of reasoning outlined above, there is a two-step process for assessing arguments. First, we need to look at the premises – do we have sufficient reason to accept them, and have we included all relevant considerations? Second, we need to look at the relationship between the premises and the conclusions. Do the premises actually provide support for the conclusion, or as is often put, does the conclusion follow from the premises? A good argument, then, is one that contains only premises that we have good reason to accept, and all such premises that are relevant to the issue at hand, and where the conclusion does follow from those premises.

Many[4] moral theories purport to help us in both theoretical and practical reasoning about moral matters. Utilitarianism,[5] for example, may guide us to the conclusions that it is both true that the action of the Good Samaritan in the biblical story was morally good because it created more happiness than any alternative action that was available to the Samaritan (a piece of theoretical reasoning), and that the Samaritan ought to have helped the stranger because doing so created more happiness than any available alternative action (a piece of practical reasoning). Moreover, if moral beliefs can themselves be motivating, then the conclusion of a piece of theoretical reasoning (such as the belief that is wrong to lie) can itself become a practical reason.

As mentioned earlier, there is a variety of different sorts of value, including moral and prudential values and, at least on the face of things, it appears inevitable that on occasion these different considerations will compete. If we try to act in such a way as to promote an outcome that is valuable in one way – (say) in terms of promoting our self-interest – we may make it impossible to act in a way that

4 Many, although not all, since some moral theories – so-called non-cognitivist theories – hold that moral claims are not, strictly speaking, true (or false), hence are not matters that are open to theoretical reasoning.

5 See John Stuart Mill, *Utilitarianism* (any edition).

will bring about an outcome that is valuable in another way – fulfilling our moral obligations, for example – and vice versa. In such situations we are faced with a conflict between two different sorts of practical reasons, deriving from two (and sometimes more than two) different kinds of value or principle.

Above, we presented an argument that the person had reasons to tell the truth, as provided by the principle not to tell lies. These reasons were moral reasons. But it is also the case that there was a reason not to tell the truth provided by the consideration of combating fraud.

In the light of this sort of conflict, a decision must be made as to which kind of reason is the more compelling. How is this to be done? Some people think that moral considerations should always take precedence over other sorts of values when there is a conflict between them. This seems implausible, however. We can certainly imagine circumstances in which the performance of a self-interested action results in the production of more value than the moral costs of failing to perform the morally right action. Consider a case where you are stopped by a stranger who, slightly distressed, asks you for directions. Knowing that there are other people who can provide these directions, and knowing also that you will miss your train to the last showing of a film you very much want to see, it seems that the prudent course of action is to ignore (politely) the needs of the stranger. In such a case, more value is promoted by acting out of self-interest rather than acting in the interests of the stranger.

Not only are there cases of practical reasoning where decision-making is difficult because the reasons derived from different values pull us in different directions, we can, it seems, find ourselves facing situations where reasons derived from the same kind of value can come into conflict. For example, it is not uncommon for us to find that we seem to have a moral reason to do a certain action, and also a moral reason not to do that action. This kind of situation, where we have moral reasons to act in two incompatible ways, is often described as a moral dilemma. Consider our above-described example of lying to the fraudster.

Much of the difference between various moral theories comes down to disagreements about what kinds of considerations are in fact relevant in practical reasoning about moral matters. Utilitarians, for example, think that the only kinds of considerations that should be taken into account are those that bear on the consequences of actions. By contrast, some deontologists, e.g. some Kantians,[6] would say that these consequences should not be given any weight – all that matters is compliance with moral principles, e.g. doing one's duty (or duties).

On the kind of pluralist approach favoured in this work, there is a whole range of different kinds of reasons that can be relevant to moral decisions and which should be taken into account in making such decisions. These will include duties and consequences, but may also include (reflectively endorsed) emotions, desires and the like.

---

6 Immanuel Kant, *Groundwork to the Metaphysics of Morals* (any edition).

Corruption, Law and Morality

Many people conflate law and morality – they think everything that is law is morally good, and that everything that is morally good is the law. More specifically, they hold that corruption is to be understood as a form of illegality, and that an act, by virtue of being unlawful, is an act of corruption. This view is particularly common among people whose task it is to make or uphold the law, such as lawyers and police officers. It is, however, a view that should be resisted. We need to insist on the distinction between law and morality and, within morality, between corruption and other species of immorality.

We should note firstly that not all laws are good. This is probably most clear in the case of repressive states such as Nazi Germany or South Africa in the apartheid era. In these states, laws were framed that discriminated against people on racial grounds. For example, blacks could not vote or own property. These regimes passed many laws that were properly framed, yet morally abhorrent. Secondly, not all morally good actions are legally enforced. Parents should be kind to their children, but there is no law to this effect.

So law and morality are not necessarily the same thing. From this it follows that sometimes the requirements of law and morality can pull us in opposite directions. This potential conflict raises issues of profound importance. Consider the laws prohibiting voluntary euthanasia or mandatory sentencing of juveniles for minor crimes. Should doctors engage in voluntary euthanasia on some occasions? There is evidence that some do, and in violation of the law. What of judges, lawyers and police in relation to crimes they know are subject to mandatory sentencing? Should they seek to bend or thwart the law on occasion?

Notwithstanding the fact that law and morality are not necessarily the same thing, it is nevertheless true – at least in the case of the criminal law – that law and morality often coincide. For example, there are laws against theft, fraud, assault and murder, and theft, fraud, assault and murder are morally wrong. This coincidence or overlap between much of the criminal law and some moral principles is no accident. The criminal law is fundamentally about ensuring minimum moral standards; it is about the protection of basic moral rights, including the right to life, to liberty, to physical security and to property. The moral rights enshrined in criminal law are those regarded as fundamental by the wider society; they constitute the basic moral norms of the society. Naturally, some of these are contentious, and as society undergoes change some of these moral norms change – for example, moral attitudes in relation to homosexuality have changed – but there is a core of moral norms which there is reason to believe will never change or ought not to change, e.g. the right to life, freedom of thought and speech, and the right to physical security.

Now let us consider corruption. The causes and effects of corruption, and how to combat corruption, are issues that are increasingly on the national and international agendas of politicians and other policymakers.[7] For example, the World Bank has relatively recently come around to the view that economic development is closely linked to corruption reduction.[8] However, most of these definitions of corruption are unsatisfactory in fairly obvious ways.

Consider one of the most popular of these definitions, namely, 'Corruption is the abuse of power by a public official for private gain.'[9] No doubt the abuse of public offices for private gain is paradigmatic of corruption. But when a bettor bribes a boxer to 'throw' a fight this is corruption for private gain, but it need not involve any public office holder; the roles of boxer and bettor are usually not public offices.

One response to this is to distinguish public corruption from private corruption, and to argue that the above definition is a definition only of public corruption. But if ordinary citizens lie when they give testimony in court, this is corruption; it is corruption of the criminal justice system. However, it does not involve abuse of a public office by a public official. And when police fabricate evidence out of a misplaced sense of justice, this is corruption of a public office, but not for private gain.

In the light of the failure of such analytical-style definitions it is tempting to try to sidestep the problem of providing a theoretical account of the concept of corruption by simply identifying corruption with specific legal and/or moral offences.

However, attempts to identify corruption with specific legal – or for that matter, moral – offences are unlikely to succeed. Perhaps the most plausible candidate is bribery; bribery is regarded by some as the quintessential form of corruption.[10] But what of nepotism? Surely it is also a paradigmatic form of corruption, and one that is conceptually distinct from bribery. The person who accepts a bribe is understood as being required to provide a benefit to the briber, otherwise it is not a bribe; but the person who is the beneficiary of an act of nepotism is not necessarily understood as being required to return the favour.

In fact, corruption is exemplified by a very wide and diverse array of phenomena of which bribery is only one kind, and nepotism another. Paradigm cases of corruption include the following. The commissioner of taxation channels public monies into his personal bank account, thereby corrupting the public financial

7 An earlier version of the material in this introduction is to be found in Miller, S., 'Corruption', *Stanford Encylopedia of Philosophy*, Summer edition, 2005. Elements also appeared in Miller, S., Roberts, P., and Spence, E., *Corruption and Anti-Corruption*, Saddle River, NJ: Prentice Hall, 2005, Chapter 1.

8 World Bank, *Helping Countries Combat Corruption*, Washington DC: World Bank, 1997.

9 For one of the most influential statements of the abuse of public office for private gain definitions see Nye, J., 'Corruption and Political Development', *American Political Science Review*, vol. 61, no. 2, 1967, pp. 417–427.

10 Noonan, J.T., *Bribes*, New York: Macmillan, 1984.

system. A political party secures a majority vote by arranging for ballot boxes to be stuffed with false voting papers, thereby corrupting the electoral process. A police officer fabricates evidence in order to secure convictions, thereby corrupting the judicial process. A number of doctors close ranks and refuse to testify against a colleague who they know has been negligent in relation to an unsuccessful surgical operation leading to loss of life; institutional accountability procedures are thereby undermined. A sports trainer provides the athletes he trains with banned substances in order to enhance their performance, thereby subverting the institutional rules laid down to ensure fair competition. It is self-evident that none of these corrupt actions are instances of bribery.

Further, it is far from obvious that the way forward at this point is simply to add a few additional offences to the initial 'list' consisting of the single offence of bribery. Candidates for being added to the list of offences would include nepotism, police fabricating evidence, cheating in sport by using drugs, fraudulent use of travel funds by politicians, and so on. However, there is bound to be disagreement in relation to any such list. For example, law enforcement practitioners often distinguish between fraud, on the one hand, and corruption on the other. Most important, any such list needs to be justified by recourse to some principle or principles. Ultimately, naming a set of offences that might be regarded as instances of corruption does not obviate the need for a theoretical, or quasi-theoretical, account of the concept of corruption.

As it happens, there is at least one further salient strategy for demarcating the boundaries of corrupt acts. Implicit in much of the literature on corruption is the view that corruption is essentially a legal offence, and essentially a legal offence in the economic sphere.[11] Accordingly, one could seek to identify corruption with economic crimes, such as bribery, fraud, and insider trading. To some extent this kind of view reflects the dominance of economically focused material in the corpus of academic literature on corruption. It also reflects the preponderance of proposed economic solutions to the problem of corruption. After all, if corruption is essentially an economic phenomenon, is it not plausible that the remedies for corruption will be economic ones?

But many acts of corruption are not unlawful. That paradigm of corruption, bribery, is a case in point. Prior to 1977 it was not unlawful for US companies to offer bribes to secure foreign contracts; indeed, elsewhere such bribery was not unlawful until much later.[12] So corruption is not necessarily unlawful.

---

11 This is implicit in much of Susan Rose-Ackerman's influential work on corruption. See Rose-Ackerman, S., *Corruption and Government*, Cambridge: Cambridge University Press, 1999.

12 See the Foreign Corrupt Practices Act of 1977, Public Law 95-213 (5305), December 19, 1977, United States Code 78a, Section 103. See also Organisation for Economic Co-operation and Development (OECD), *Convention Against Bribery of Foreign Public Officials in International Business Transactions*, 15 February 1999.

This is because corruption is not, at bottom, simply a matter of law; rather it is fundamentally a matter of morality.

Secondly, corruption is not necessarily economic in character. An academic who plagiarizes the work of others is not committing an economic crime or misdemeanour; and she might be committing plagiarism simply in order to increase her academic status. There might not be any financial benefit sought or gained. Academics are more strongly motivated by status than by wealth. A police officer who fabricates evidence against a person he believes to be guilty of paedophilia is not committing an economic crime; and he might do so because he believes the accused to be guilty, and does not want him to go unpunished. Economics is not necessarily involved as an element of the officer's crime or as a motivation. When police do wrong they are often motivated by a misplaced sense of justice, rather than by financial reward. Again, a person in authority motivated by sadistic pleasure who abuses her power by meting out cruel and unjust treatment to those subject to her authority is not engaging in an economic crime; and she is not motivated by economic considerations. Many of those who occupy positions of authority are motivated by a desire to exercise power for its own sake, rather than by a desire for financial reward.

Economic corruption is an important form of corruption; however, it is not the only form of corruption. There are non-economic forms of corruption, including many types of police corruption, judicial corruption, political corruption, academic corruption, and so on. Indeed, there are at least as many forms of corruption as there are human institutions that might become corrupted. Further, economic gain is not the only motivation for corruption. There are a variety of different kinds of attractions that motivate corruption. These include status, power, addiction to drugs or gambling, and sexual gratification, as well as economic gain.

We can conclude that the various currently influential definitions of corruption, and the recent attempts to circumscribe corruption by listing paradigmatic offences, have failed. They failed in large part because the class of corrupt actions comprises an extremely diverse array of types of moral and legal offences.

The notion of a corrupt action presupposes the prior notion of an uncorrupted and morally legitimate process, role or institution, or perhaps of an uncorrupted and morally worthy person. That is, the act of corruption brings about, or contributes to bringing about, a corrupt condition of something or someone, and the two principal objects of corruption are institutions and persons. Let us refer to the corruption of institutions as institutional corruption, and the corruption of the moral character of persons as personal corruption. One important focus in this book is on a species of institutional corruption, namely corruption on the part of occupational role occupants. However, it goes without saying that since institutions are comprised of persons, institutional corruption and personal corruption are interdependent. Specifically, institutional roles are occupied by persons, so the corruption of a person qua institutional role occupant is institutional corruption.

The condition of corruption exists only relative to: (1) an uncorrupted condition, which condition is (2) that of being a morally legitimate process, role or institution, or that of being a morally worthy person. Consider the uncorrupted judicial process. It consists of the presentation of objective evidence that has been gathered lawfully, of testimony in court being presented truthfully, of the rights of the accused being respected, and so on. This otherwise morally legitimate judicial process is corrupted if one or more of its constitutive actions are not performed in accordance with the process as it is rightly intended to be. Thus, to present fabricated evidence, to lie on oath, and so on, are all potentially corrupt actions. Now consider the uncorrupted tendering process. It consists of a fair, competitive process – a morally legitimate process – whereby the tender is awarded to the person or organization that will do the job well and at the lowest price. This tendering process is corrupted if the job is awarded, not on the basis of merit, but on the basis of a bribe, or if one of the tenderers is given inside knowledge of the price being offered by the others.

So an action is corrupt by virtue of the effects it has; specifically, it corrupts something or someone. In short, corruption is a *causal* concept.

Moreover, the corrupt condition of the person or thing corrupted exists only relative to some moral standard(s) which is definitional of the uncorrupted condition of that thing or person. The moral standards in question might be minimum moral standards, or they might be ideals. Corruption in a tendering process is a failure to comply with minimum moral standards enshrined in laws or regulations. On the other hand, gradual loss of innocence might be a process of corruption relative to an ideal state. In short, corruption is a *moral* concept (albeit, in the sense of being a species of *im*morality).

Occupational Ethics

The task of occupational ethics – as a branch of ethics, and thus in turn of applied philosophy – is to reason systematically and make judgements about ethical issues and problems that arise for members of occupational groups.

As we saw above, in this context 'to reason' is to be understood broadly. To reason in this sense includes, but is not exhausted by, deductive reasoning. And to reason about occupational ethics is not necessarily to generate abstract truths that are good for all people in all places at all times. There are some moral propositions that are universal, e.g. do not murder innocent persons. However, many of the propositions of occupational ethics need to be relativized to particular institutions and occupations. Physical courage might be a necessary virtue for police, but not for academics. Such relativization in respect of ethical claims about occupational practices and institutions has been part of philosophizing from the time of the philosophers, Aristotle through Hume, Rousseau, Hegel, and up to modern times.

This need for relativization to context has nothing whatsoever to do with the opposition to objective truth propounded in the past by philosophers such as Nietzsche, and more recently by postmodernists and others. A claim once relativized to context still needs to be assessed for its truth/falsity. In occupational ethics, the need for relativization arises in part because the ethical dimension of any given occupational practice has what might be called an internal and an external aspect.

Two things need to be noted about the external ethical aspect. First, it consists of moral principles that ought to be adhered to by the occupant of the occupational role, and by people in general. For example, members of occupational groups (and people in general) ought not to commit murder or theft. But secondly, these moral principles are typically not sufficient for the person to undertake that role competently. Merely because an accountant is not a murderer or thief etc. does not make him or her a competent accountant.

These external moral principles – and their associated character traits (virtues) – have such a high degree of generality that they exist more or less independently of any particular occupational practice. Such principles and virtues govern behaviour and attitudes in most occupational behaviour; for example, the principle not to take human life, or the virtue of honesty. Many such moral principles are enshrined in the law. Thus, it is against the law to commit murder or assault, to steal or to engage in fraud.

That said, there are many external moral principles that are not, or should not be, enshrined in the law. For example, cheating on one's sexual partner is regarded as a vice, as is failing to keep one's promises.

The internal ethical aspect consists of principles and virtues that are necessary for a person to undertake his or her particular occupational practice competently. Thus, good hand/eye coordination is a virtue that is internal to being a good pilot, but by no means to most occupations.

This is not to say that all aspects of professional practice are matters of morality. That would be absurd. It might be unprofessional for lawyers to wear shabby clothing when appearing in court of for doctors to be unsympathetic to their patients, but it is not necessarily immoral.

Moreover, possession of specific technical skills and knowledge might be necessary for someone to perform an occupational role successfully, and therefore undertaking a role when one does not possess those skills or knowledge might be a breach of ethics. For one thing, undertaking the role without the necessary skills may cause harm. For another, it may constitute deception, if (say) one's clients falsely believe that one has the skills in question.

That said, possession of a technical skill, or of technical knowledge, does not in general confer a moral or ethical status. Being able to lay carpets does not in itself make carpet laying a morally virtuous activity. On the other hand, we regard some occupational roles as important by virtue of the moral goods that they bring about, e.g. doctors can save lives. Accordingly, we regard possession of the skills necessary to perform these roles – roles that realize moral goods – as moral or ethical virtues.

Some practices that are internal to a given occupation are matters of morality, and not because they violate some externally determined moral principle. For example, if a policeman fails to intervene in an attempted burglary, the policeman has not only failed in his professional duty, he is also morally culpable. Similarly, a doctor is morally culpable if she fails to attend to a patient who is very ill. And a correctional officer who is negligent with respect to the security of prisoners in his/her charge is morally culpable; similarly for a nurse with respect to patients in his/her care.

Thus, in undertaking a particular occupation, individuals typically accept professional obligations, but some of these obligations are also moral obligations. These moral obligations are additional to the moral obligations that they had prior to entering the occupation; they are internal to the occupation.

Designing-in Ethics

In relation to some of the practical ethical issues, the problem lies more, so to speak, at the level of will than at the level of intellect.[13] In the case of some such problems there is no particular intellectual confusion about whether the actions or policies in question are morally right or morally wrong. Rather, the problem is how to prevent or contain manifest wrongdoing, and how to promote virtue. Consider gross corruption. We all know, or should know, that the fraudulent transfer of billions of dollars from Russian banks into the accounts of criminals in the USA[14] constituted wholesale theft of the savings of millions of Russian citizens, and was morally wrong; the problem is how to prevent such corruption and, more generally, how to promote integrity in institutions.

On the other hand, many of the ethical problems that we confront involve genuine intellectual confusion and dispute in relation to the morality of the actions or policies themselves. Consider euthanasia, abortion or the ethical problems that have arisen, and continue to arise, in the context of new scientific and technological developments. The degree of controversy would seem to indicate that it is far from self-evident whether, and to what extent, genetically modified foods ought to be produced, or what forms, if any, of cloning or human enhancement are morally acceptable, and if so, for what purposes.

We have distinguished between two kinds of ethical problems; those at the level of will and those at the level of intellect. However, it must also be stressed that manifest wrongdoing – a problem at the level of will – when it takes place on a large scale, or is complex in character, typically gives rise to intellectual problems, including intellectually problematic ethical dilemmas. Consider a rising crime rate. Crime is morally wrong, therefore we must combat crime. So far so good. But obvious measures such as harsher penalties, or incarcerating large numbers of offenders may not solve the problem, and in any case give rise to additional

---

13 See Miller, S., 'Research in Applied Ethics: Problems and Perspectives', *Philosophia*, vol. 37, no. 2, 2009, pp. 185–201.

14 'Russian money launderers plead guilty', at http://news.bbc.co.uk/2/hi/americas/645717.stm (last accessed 21 August 2009).

ethical problems. Harsh penalties or mandatory sentencing may violate principles of justice. Prisons are expensive, and may simply serve as incubators of crime.

Certainly, an appropriate balance often needs to be struck between (say), on the one hand, the benefits of providing law enforcement agencies with greater powers, and, on the other, the rights of suspects and offenders.

In cases where there is no moral balance to be struck between salient available options, or where all options are unsatisfactory, e.g. whether or not to increase regulation at the expense of economic efficiency or allow corruption to thrive, there is a need for creative thinking; a third option must be designed. This third option might be a single new practice or invention, e.g. 'turning' of the members of criminal organizations, negotiated prosecutions, miniature cameras, following money trails.

Design products, both institutional and technological, are all around us. They include highway systems, rail transportation systems, cars, tax systems, laws and regulatory frameworks, schools, universities, hospitals, corporations, business processes, clinical protocols, computer programs, household appliances, streets and squares, public buildings and houses. More and more people live in these extensively designed and engineered environments. Design is a ubiquitous feature of our contemporary world.

These institutional and technological contrivances empower us in a myriad of ways. They bring buyers and sellers together (markets), they educate us (schools), they provide us with transport (motorcars), and allow us to communicate over long distances instantaneously (mobile phones).

However, these very same humanly designed institutions and technologies also constrain our freedom to act. Motorways enable us to travel speedily by car from A to B; but motorways also require us to drive on one side of the road and along a predetermined pathway between A and B. The institution of the police enables us to conduct our daily business safely and without unwarranted interference; but equally the police constrain our activities in the public domain to do as we see fit.

So design products are ubiquitous; indeed, in part, constitutive of our human environments. And they empower us and constrain us. As such, design products have an important ethico-normative dimension. Hospitals and pacemakers enable us to save and prolong life. On the other hand, military organizations and weapons of mass destruction allow us to destroy lives. Indeed, quite frequently institutions and technologies have dual uses, ethically speaking: they can be used for good, but they can also be used for evil. Consider techniques for genetic engineering or the modern corporation.

Sometimes a moral end or moral feature is designed into an institution or technology; sometimes a morally desirable outcome is the fortuitous, but unintended, consequence of an institutional arrangement or technological invention. A paradigm case of a morally objectionable end being designed into an artefact was Robert Moses' low hanging overpasses in New York, which were intended to prevent the buses from the poor black neighbourhoods being routed to the beaches near New York – a favourite destination of white middle-class families. This notion of designing in ethics is complex and elusive. In what sense, for example, are the ethical ends or moral aspects of hospitals or pacemakers a constitutive feature of these entities? And in what sense is there a designer? Institutions, for example, are typically the result of the actions of multiple agents interacting over generations. A further issue pertains to the conceptual, practical and moral limits on design. Here, it is especially important to note the moral limits on notions of designing or redesigning human beings per se. Some recent discussions on human enhancement, for example, offer a brave new world of future 'super-humans' with greatly enhanced sensory apparatus and possessed of prodigious memories and calculative capacities. The underlying conception of a human being informing some of the more glib pronouncements made in this connection is that of a computerized robot – a conception that is as facile as it is dangerous.

At any rate, one set of concerns is with these and other theoretical issues. A second set of concerns pertains to various instances of *designing ethics* into institutions and technology.

Hitherto, the study of ethics has tended to focus on the analysis of pre-existing concepts, and the adjudication between predetermined options – such adjudication often being understood in terms of a process of weighing up the moral considerations inherent in these given options. By contrast, a more recent favoured approach to the study of contemporary ethical issues, which (following Jeroen van den Hoven[15]) we will refer to as 'designing in ethics', emphasizes the need to create or expose additional options and, thereby, reconfigure or re-design the option set.

As van den Hoven points out, this design turn in applied ethics is the third and the most recent phase in the development of contemporary ethics. After an almost exclusive focus on meta-ethics at the beginning of the 20th century, there was an applied turn in the latter decades of the 20th century. However, this applied turn consisted of the application of existing theory to practical problems, and involved primarily the above-described static process of adjudication between pre-existing options.

By contrast, we are insisting on the need to identify and articulate a rather different category of questions in applied ethics. It is not simply a matter of this familiar type of question: 'Given this situation and given the fact that there are two options A and B open to the individual chooser (e.g. chooser in a prisoner's dilemma scenario, chooser in a Judith Jarvis Thomson trolley scenario) what should she do?' For we also need to focus on the following type of question: 'How can we redesign the option set such that there is another option C – an option that is additional to the currently existing options A and B?' Crucially, option C meets all our ethical requirements and does not force us to choose between them.

Gradually applied moral philosophers working on real life problems are coming to realize the possibility and importance of designing-in ethics to institutional

15 Van den Hoven, J., 'Computer Ethics and Moral Methodology', *Metaphilosophy*, vol. 28, no. 3, 1997, pp. 234–249.

arrangements, such as economic incentive structures and legal frameworks, and to technical and engineering artefacts and infrastructures, such as surveillance systems and computer programs. Here, the key point is that moral philosophers need to be part of the process of designing institutional arrangements and new technologies. In this book we seek to make a contribution to the designing-in ethics enterprise by designing the broad contours of an integrity system[16] for occupational groups.

An integrity system, as we use the term in this book, is an assemblage of institutional entities, roles, mechanisms and procedures, the purpose of which is to ensure compliance with minimum ethical standards and to promote the pursuit of ethical goals.

Here, we note that although regulatory frameworks and integrity systems typically overlap – and ought to be mutually reinforcing – they are not identical notions. This is because a regulatory framework is a structured set of explicit laws, rules or regulations governing behaviour, issued by some institutional authority and backed by sanctions.

In Chapter 2 we elaborate our account of integrity systems. First, however, we need to focus our attention on an important object of such systems, namely, occupational groups.

---

16 See, for example, Sampford, C., Smith, R., and Brown, A.J., 'From Greek Temple to Bird's Nest: Towards a Theory of Coherence and Mutual Accountability for National Integrity Systems', *Australian Journal of Public Administration*, vol. 64, no. 2, 2005, pp. 96–108.

Chapter 1
Professionalization and Occupations

Professions and Occupations

In this chapter, our concern is with occupational and professional roles.[1] Shortly, we will distinguish professional roles from other occupational roles. However, first we need to be clear on the notion of an occupational (or professional) role. Roles are teleological in nature; they are distinguished from one another according to the ends or goals they serve.[2] Thus, we distinguish the role of a police officer from that of a chef by virtue of the different ends that they serve; police officers act in order to ensure law and order, chefs act in order to provide cuisine.

While it is necessary to differentiate roles, the telos – or end – of a role is not sufficient to distinguish one role from another. Perhaps the end of lawyers, like that of police, is to ensure that the law is upheld. Accordingly, we also need to attend to the means or type of action or activity by which the end of some occupational role is realized. Police, but not lawyers, uphold the law by means of the use, or threat of the use, of coercive force.

So occupational roles are defined in part by the end or ends that they serve, and in part by the types of action or activities that they perform, which are the means to the end(s). In addition, some roles are evidently in part defined by the attitude that practitioners ought to have or adopt. This seems to be true of the caring occupations, e.g. child-minders, nurses, social workers, psychologists.

Historically, a further distinction has been made between occupations and professions. All professional roles are occupational roles, but not all occupational roles are professional roles.

The terms 'professional' and 'profession' are of course used in a wide variety of ways – we take medicine to be a profession, but also, it would seem, prostitution; we speak of lawyers acting in a professional manner, but we might also say of a carpet-layer that he has done a very professional job.[3] Here, however, we use the

1 The following account of professional roles is taken from Alexandra, A., and Miller, S., 'Needs, Moral Self-consciousness and Professional Roles', *Professional Ethics*, vol. 5, nos. 1 & 2, 1996, pp. 43–61.

2 Miller, S., *Social Action: A Teleological Account*, New York: Cambridge University Press, 2001, Chapter 1, and Miller, S., *The Moral Foundations of Social Institutions: A Philosophical Study*, New York: Cambridge University Press, 2009, Chapter 2.

3 For a useful survey of different approaches to the definition of professions see Barker, S., 'What is a Profession?' *Professional Ethics*, vol. 1, nos. 1&2, 1992, pp. 73–99. Barker also propounds his own quasi-contractual account.

terms 'professional' and 'profession' in a relatively restricted way. Our approach to the issue of professional roles involves an investigation of, and generalization from, the characteristic features of such paradigmatic professions as the law, medicine and architecture, and we take it that a person counts as a professional by virtue of their membership of such a profession. Despite regional variations in the organization of, and constraints on, professional work, there is nevertheless a perhaps surprising degree of congruence in such matters, at least in the English-speaking world.

As noted above, a worker will be classified as a member of a particular occupation by virtue of the characteristic activities that they undertake, taken together with the end that those activities serve – gardeners are just those people who tend gardens, cooks those who prepare food, and so on. Likewise, professionals can be identified in part by recourse to the characteristic activities that they perform, and the ends that these activities serve: doctors are just those workers who heal the sick, lawyers those who give legal advice, architects those who design buildings, engineers those who construct buildings, and so on. Such a definition of professionals and professions seems adequate for some of the things that are called as such, such as prostitution, but will not do for the objects of our attention – what we have dubbed the paradigmatic professions. This can be seen by reflecting on the fact that the paid performance of these functions does not necessarily qualify the performer as a professional. To earn that description, the performer also needs to bear various distinguishing social and legal marks. Typically, they have to possess certain educational qualifications, belong to the appropriate professional body and so on.

Indeed, there is a large degree of consensus in the sociological and philosophical literature as to the distinguishing marks of professional occupations.[4] Five such marks are especially salient. An occupational group counts as a profession by virtue of its having the following features: the work of its members is oriented to the provision of some good; members of the group possess and exercise creative expertise in the provision of this good; they possess a high degree of autonomy in the exercise of their expertise; they are grouped together as a self-conscious community; and they have a certain institutional status that typically is accorded legal recognition and protection. Let us elaborate further on these distinctive marks of the professions.

First, there is the end of the professions. In one view, the goods towards which the work of members of a professional group ought to be oriented are certain fundamental ethical goods, such as justice and health. Moreover, those who need the fundamental goods in question typically cannot themselves provide them, or at least cannot provide them without assistance. In modern societies, the providers

4 Other marks, such as self-regulation, are more controversial. See for example Bayles, M.D., 'Professional Power and Self-Regulation', *Business and Professional Ethics Journal*, vol. 5, no. 2, 1986, p. 27; Camenisch, P., 'Business Ethics: On Getting to the Heart of the Matter', *Business and Professional Ethics Journal*, vol. 1, no. 1, 1981, p. 61.

of these goods will often be professionals and professionals have a moral duty to provide these good to those who need them (see the section 'The Moral Basis of Professional Duties' below).

Second, the successful prosecution of professional work requires expertise based on a body of specialized knowledge and, therefore, extensive and ongoing, training and education. Moreover, professionals typically require fineness of judgement in the application of this knowledge. These qualities are necessary because of the complexity and yet indeterminate nature of much of a professional's work. There is, for example, typically no mechanical procedure available to guide the decision as to what is the most appropriate means to the desired end. Consider the work of an architect.

Third, the characteristic skilled creativity of the professional entails a consequent substantial degree of professional autonomy (see the final section of this chapter). With respect to a range of important decisions – for example, whether or not to perform a surgical operation and by what method – the professional is the one to decide, and not (say) the professional's manager.

Fourth, the skills of the professional can only be developed and transmitted within a group. Professional groups are structured as networks in the sense of economic organizations that exchange goods without explicit equity investment or ownership.[5] Professions constitute a community of practitioners who operate separately – indeed often in competition with each other – for many purposes, but are nevertheless dependent on each other for the maintenance and development of their core competencies, and for access to knowledge and expertise. Professionals typically undergo a lengthy, and often ongoing, process of training and accreditation by their fellows. Given the indeterminacy and complexity of much professional work – hence the need for professional autonomy – new knowledge is likely to be generated by individual practitioners in the course of their work, and then transmitted to other members of the network. A doctor, for example, might learn of new developments in his field from a colleague, or seek the professional opinion of other doctors when she is not sure what to make of a puzzling case. And professionals will often depend on references from other professionals for business.

Fifth, the paradigmatic professions, as well as being networked communities in this sense are also institutional entities of a certain sort: members of the profession belong to professional bodies such as the Australian Medical Association.[6] The

5 See Savage, D.A. 'The Professions in Theory and History: The Case of Pharmacy', *Business and Economic History*, vol. 23, 1994, pp. 129–160.

6 There are interesting points of divergence and convergence between professional associations and industrial unions. The latter have been conceived simply as organizations acting in the interest of their members, the former as having a role in relation to the community interest, so to speak, in the services provided by the member. In recent times some trade unions have sought to carve out a role not dissimilar to that of a professional association, e.g. the National Tertiary Education Union in Australia.

modern professions are typically groups with venerable historical roots, and organizationally they are often continuous with the medieval guilds. Nevertheless, in the institutional form with which we are familiar, they are very much a modern phenomenon. In his study, *The Medical Profession in Mid-Victorian England*, M.J. Peterson argues, for example, that it was impossible to talk of the medical profession in England at all before the Medical Act of 1858, and even then of dubious value for a considerable time after that.[7] What is distinctive, in the first place, about the modern institutions, as against their historical forebears, is their relation to the state – they are legally defined institutions, which is not to say that they are totally constituted by the law.

Therefore a profession comprises persons who are not simply practitioners, but who occupy specific positions and stand in authority relations to others in a structured professional organization and pursue the collective ends of that organization, through such activities as lobbying the government, accrediting individuals and institutions, disciplining miscreant members, as well as ensuring that sufficient practitioners to service the whole community are trained and licensed, and that remuneration for such practitioners is sufficiently attractive to make it likely that they will actually exercise their skills, and so on.

Not only are members of the paradigmatic professions organized into such institutions, it is at least arguable that they *should* be so organized. Such organization facilitates the achievement of the collective ends of the members of the profession. Members of the profession are well placed to identify the means to the provision of the fundamental goods definitive of that profession as well as the standards and norms of professional behaviour that facilitate the achievement of those goods. The provision of these goods may require actions that reach beyond the provision of service to individuals. The achievement and retention of health is the end of the health professions, for instance. But reaching this end is dependent, in part, on the provision of adequate public health facilities, such as a clean water supply, and an effective sewerage service. As part of their professional role, doctors should be prepared to agitate for such services. Although they can do so as individual members of the profession, they can do so much more effectively as an institution. It is important, then, that professional institutions have an independence from direct political or industrial control, and indeed the capacity to interact with and influence organs of state and commercial power. Moreover, to

---

7 Peterson, M.J., *The Medical Profession in Mid-Victorian England*, Berkeley: University of California Press, 1978; cf. Willis, E. *Medical Dominance*, Sydney: Allen and Unwin, 1990, pp. 37–38. The standard account of the rise of the modern professions is Carr-Saunders, A.M., and Wilson, P.A., *The Professions*, Oxford: Clarendon Press, 1933. The achievement of governmental recognition and protection was not an easy or uninterrupted process: for an account of some of the vicissitudes encountered by the professions in 19th-century America see Friedson, E., 'Nourishing Professionalism', in E.D. Pelligrino, R.M. Veatch, and J.P. Langan (eds), *Ethics, Trust and the Professions: Philosophical and Cultural Aspects*, Washington, DC: Georgetown University Press, 1991, pp. 193–215, esp. p. 196.

the extent to which professional institutions are particularly well-placed to identify and enforce appropriate standards and norms of professional behaviour they have a claim to possess self-regulatory powers, and to have input into the design of external regulatory regimes (we discuss professional self-regulation further in the final section of this chapter).

If, indeed, the professions are a distinctive form of occupation with the defining features described above then this will need to be reflected in the various elements of integrity systems constructed to guide them. For example, since the telos – or end – of the work of the professions is a moral good, this should to be stressed in their codes of ethics, as should the distinctive rights of professional practitioners, e.g. professional autonomy. Again, given the role of the professional associations, the codes of ethics of members of the professions will need to have sanctions built into them (see chapters three and four).

We have argued for a distinction between the professions and other occupations. That said, there is no clear dividing line between the professions and other occupations. Rather, there is a set of criteria for being a profession. Many occupations meet some of these criteria, but not all; so they are not professions. Some occupations are such that most of their members meet the criteria; so these are professions. However, some members of these occupations – the occupations that meet the criteria for being professions – do not meet all of the criteria. So there are grey areas. But here, as elsewhere, the existence of greyness does not destroy the distinction between black and white.

The Professions and the Market

The achievement of the institutional status of a professional brings with it a set of rights and duties that are, in a variety of ways, anomalous in comparison to those held by other workers: this anomalous status is in part a consequence of the legal privileges and requirements extended to the profession. Of great importance in this connection is the relationship of the professional to the market.

Historically, professionals have been sheltered in important ways from the disciplines imposed on other occupational groups by market forces. Professions have exercised a legal monopoly or near monopoly (in the case of, for example, lawyers) or a kind of quasi-monopoly (in the case of most other professions) over the provision of services in their area of expertise. There have been at least strong disincentives put in the way of non-professionals entering the market in such services: they have not been allowed to sue for fees owed, for example, and they have not been allowed access to many of the institutional settings where such services are required, irrespective of the wishes of those who consume the services. For example only qualified lawyers can represent others in court for payment,[8] and only qualified medical practitioners can treat people in hospitals. Not only

8 See the Victorian Legal Profession Practices Act 1958.

have professionals been sheltered from competition with non-professionals, their exercise of the control they are granted as a group over entry into the profession (often called 'closure' in the sociological literature) means that they have also tended to be sheltered from vigorous competition within the profession. In such respects, then, professionals appear to have been privileged, relative to most other workers.

There is a tendency within the sociological literature to see the achievement and retention of such privileges as the end of professional organization; and correspondingly to take the attribution of the status of a profession to some occupational grouping as a function of such achievement. In other words a group is counted as a profession because it is privileged, not privileged because it is a profession.[9] However, this is only part of the story about the distinctive status of professionals. For if it is true that, in some respects, professionals are privileged relative to other workers, it is also true that in other respects professionals are restricted relative to other workers.

As we have claimed, professionals have been sheltered from the full rigours of the market. It is also the case, however, that they have been denied full access to the potential benefits of the market. Typically, professionals are forbidden from profiting from their expertise in a variety of ways. Of course, they are restricted by the law, as are all workers, but it is worth noting that the consequences of using their skills for illegal ends may be more severe for professionals than for others, since the professional faces not simply the standard legal penalty associated with their wrongdoing, but also the prospect of effectively losing their right to continue to practise their occupation, or the benefits that go with practising their occupation as a member of a profession. In this respect a professional is unlike, say, the farmer who uses specialized knowledge to grow a crop of marijuana. And they may similarly be penalized even if they do things which if they were done by other people would not count as illegal. Lawyers are forbidden, for example, from engaging in action which is judged to be 'dishonourable' by a body of their professional fellows (in Victoria, Australia, a committee of the Law Institute), and may have their professional status cancelled or suspended as a consequence of such a judgment.

In some ways, professionals possess less control over the exercise of their occupational skills than most other workers. Doctors can be required to tend

---

9 See Friedson, E., 'Nourishing Professionalism', in E.D. Pelligrino, R.M. Veatch, and J.P. Langan (eds), *Ethics, Trust and the Professions: Philosophical and Cultural Aspects*, Washington, DC: Georgetown University Press, 1991, p. 197; cf. Murphy, R., *Social Closure: The Theory of Monopolization and Exclusion*, Oxford: Clarendon Press, 1988; Collins, R., 'Market Closure and the Conflict Theory of Professions', in M. Burrage, and R. Torstendahl, *Professions in Theory and History*, London: Sage Publications, 1990. For a useful survey of views in relation to this issue see Newton, L., 'The Origins of Professionalism: Sociological Conclusions and Ethical Implications', *Business and Professional Ethics Journal*, vol. 1, no. 4, 1982, pp. 33–49.

the sick and injured (when there is no other qualified practitioner available, for example) whether they want to or not. Lawyers are required to accept clients on a 'first come, first served' basis.

One of the consequences of the restrictions on the activities of professionals is that the area of discretion that professionals and their clients possess in regard to their contractual arrangements is also unusually restricted, in comparison with the degree of flexibility typically enjoyed by other service providers and their clients. If a person employs someone to paint their house it can be agreed that they will be paid less than the standard rate, in return, say, for not insisting on the usual degree of finished detail. Professionals and their clients cannot enter into agreements of this form for much of the kinds of work undertaken by professionals. (So a person cannot enter an agreement with their doctor to pay her less than the standard fee for the removal of an appendix, on the condition that she spends no more than an hour on the operation.)

We can conclude that, historically at least, professionals could not plausibly be represented as participants in the open market, negotiating the sale of the use of their skills to the highest bidder.

However, it may well be that, in this regard, things have changed, or are in the process of changing. Certainly, there is pressure on the professions from various quarters, for instance in Australia from the Australian Competition and Consumer Commission, to adopt a more competitive market-centred model. Moreover, many professionals are now employed in large business corporations, and in this context there is a tendency to see their work as no different from that of any other employee, in that it is supposed to contribute to the economic 'product' of the corporation which pays them. These forces are now so strong that in some quarters there is talk of the 'de-professionalization' of the professions. By 'de-professionalization' it is meant that the professions cannot, and perhaps ought not, be regarded as distinctive occupations.

At any rate, the question that now has to be asked is whether or not de-professionalization is a good thing; or, at least, whether it is a good thing in certain respects. Given the conception of the professions offered in the previous section, it is self-evident that de-professionalization would be a bad thing that ought to be resisted.

What is in large part at stake here is the basic conception of the professions as necessarily different from other more market-based occupations. As already noted, in one view the salient features of the professions can be understood and assessed by seeing the role of the professional as the provider of ethical goods, including catering for fundamental needs. Moreover, as argued in the next section, professionals have a duty to prove these goods, to satisfy these needs. Accordingly, standards of professional practice necessarily are often themselves moral standards.

Given this, the relation between professionals and their client group should not be assimilated to that which holds between buyers and sellers in a market. This is also the case for many other occupations. Consider police officers, soldiers, ambulance drivers and firemen. In the idealized picture of the market with which we are familiar from the writings of economists and bureaucrats, market actors – buyers and sellers alike – are driven by selfish motivations, the desire to satisfy their own desires. A transaction is rational when, and only when, each of the parties to the transaction believes, with good reason, that their desires will be more satisfied after the transaction than they were before. In this picture there is no obligation on a holder of a good to sell it if he prefers to do something else with his time, or if he judges that he will not be better off after the transaction than before.

So professionals are not simply market actors, since they do have an obligation to provide certain kinds of goods to those in need of them. This general obligation entails the demands made on particular professionals to provide their services to particular clients whether they wish to or not. It also helps explain restrictions on the contractual freedom in dealings between clients and professionals. A professional is obliged to do what is necessary for the satisfaction of a client's needs, so they are not free to enter into agreements that would prevent them from so acting. (Nevertheless, a client does retain a lot of contractual freedom since they are not forced to engage a professional; and often there are a variety of means to the satisfaction of their need, and they can negotiate with the professional so as to obtain the one they prefer.)

In the actual exercise of their skill, of course, professionals often act in ways that could hardly be represented as providing ethical goods to their clients, but rather are driven by market considerations, including consumer demand, and the desire on the part of individual professionals to maximize their financial benefits. Plastic surgeons at times perform operations the purpose of which is the gratification of the patient's vanity, lawyers in the employ of the rich use their expertise to intimidate the poor, and so on.

In addition, the very nature of both the professional community and the professional corporation often actively militates against the achievement of the satisfaction of the ends that we take to be definitive of the profession. Members of a professional community tend to develop a high degree of solidarity; a solidarity that is expressed in the difficulty in getting a member of a profession to testify to the incompetence of a fellow, and an unwillingness to expel incompetents. Moreover, the activities of professional corporations often cannot be represented as conducive to the satisfaction of individual needs, and may even be inconsistent with such satisfaction. The role of such organizations is not, as a matter of logic or fact, necessarily identical with the professional role of the individual members of the profession.

Nor are the collective ends constitutive of these organizations necessarily identical with the collective ends of the profession construed as a community. For example, particular professional bodies typically pursue the collective end of the promotion of the financial interests of their members. But such interests are not necessarily identical with the long-term interests of the professional community, and may well be inconsistent with the demands of the professional's role as we have interpreted it. Such inconsistencies are particularly likely to arise when the interests of the membership comport with the interests of some powerful external force, such as the state. For example, a government may require cutbacks in health expenditure, and as a consequence fewer medical students.[10] This may well be in the financial interests of the existing membership of the medical association – it means fewer doctors but higher incomes for those who are doctors – al though not in the interests of the health of the community. One way to guard against undue pursuit of self-interest on the part of a professional body in relation to decisions regarding entry requirements, standards, and so on, is to have appropriate external representation (see the final section of this chapter).

In conclusion, the relation between professionals – and many other like occupations – and their client group should not be assimilated to that which holds between buyers and sellers in a market. This is not to say that professionals are not, or ought not to be, in the market. In many cases they can and should be. Moreover, when professionals compete in the marketplace they ought to do so under conditions of fair competition, and with due regard to the rights of consumers. However, the professions, and other like occupations, have a larger purpose. They exist to provide moral goods, including health, education, justice and the like; and these are public goods, the provision of which is in the public interest. Where the marketplace serves as a means to this end, all is well. But when a competitive market impedes the realization of this end, then it is the competitive market that must be subjected to scrutiny and give way to strictures. Integrity systems for the professions need to address this issue, and reflect the relative priority of the moral, and public, goods that justify their existence over the requirements of the market.

The Moral Basis of Professional Duties

We have claimed that members of the professions have moral duties to their clients, e.g. fiduciary duties, that members of other occupations do not necessarily have. We now need to justify this claim.[11]

As we saw above, professionals – and their duties – cannot be understood in purely individualistic terms. Professionals are members of institutions. To understand the nature of professional role morality we need to examine the moral basis for the creation of relevant institutions and the consequent institutional moral duties to assist attaching to members of those institutions.

---

10 This is not to suggest that the interests of the state and professional groups always coincide. In fact the likelihood of conflict between these interests is quite high in some circumstances. One of the principal ends of the academic profession is the pursuit of truth, but notoriously the truths in question may be unpalatable to the state in times of political agitation.

11 Miller, S., *The Moral Foundations of Social Institutions: A Philosophical Study*, New York: Cambridge University Press, 2009, Chapter 2.

In the case of the professional role of doctor, for example, the moral basis appears to be aggregate human need – the need for health care in particular. Each member of a community has an individual human right to, say, some minimum level of health care, if he or she needs it. It is only when a certain threshold of aggregate need exists, however, that the establishment of an institution takes place; a hospital, for example, is not established because a single person's right to health care has not been realized. When such a threshold of aggregate need exists, what is required is collective or joint action on the part of many persons. Accordingly, a cooperative enterprise or institution is established that has as a collective end the provision of health care to the needy many by means of the joint activity of the doctors, nurses and other members of the health care institution.

Here, we stress the importance of the distinction between needs and desires. As David Wiggins argues, needs are not simply a class of strong desires.[12] If I desire to have *x* and *x* is *y* then I do not necessarily desire to have *y*. Assume, for example, that *x* is a glass of water and *y* is a glass of H_2O but I do not know that water is H_2O. I desire a glass of water, but I do not desire a glass of H_2O. Now consider needs. If I need *x* (water) and *x* is *y* (water is H_2O) then I need y (H_2O). Unlike 'desire', 'need' is not an intentional verb and, unlike desires, what it is that I need depends on the way the world objectively is, as opposed to how I think it is. Wiggins also points to a distinction between what he calls categorical and instrumental needs. A need is categorical when it must be fulfilled if harm to a person is to be avoided. So food is a categorical need while my need for, say, $10 so that I can go to the movies is merely an instrumental need. This non-contingent connection between needs and harms is in part reflective of the fact that many needs, and specifically basic human needs, are relative to constitutive properties of human beings. Being the kind of organisms that they are, human beings need, for example, a flow of oxygen; indeed, they cannot survive without it. Importantly, human needs are relative to human well being; relative, that is, not simply to human survival, but to human flourishing. This is not to say that any condition that contributes to human flourishing is a need. But it is to say that unless certain human needs are met – including some needs that are not strictly necessary for survival – humans cannot flourish; children, for example, evidently need to be reared in a relatively affectionate setting if they are not to suffer long-term emotional harm. The non-contingent relation between needs and harms and, more specifically, the relativity of human needs to human flourishing, implies that needs, or at least human needs, are ethically normative in character. Hence, to fulfil someone's human need is pro tanto a good thing to do, and to deprive someone of his or her human need is pro tanto a bad thing to do. Moreover, given this normative character of human needs, human needs can generate, albeit only under certain conditions, moral rights and moral obligations. Whether or not a human need generates a moral right to the thing needed will depend, for example, on the extent of the harm suffered if the

12 Wiggins, D., 'Claims of Need', in D. Wiggins, *Needs, Values, Truth: Essays in the Philosophy of Value*, 2nd edn, Oxford: Blackwell, 1991, pp. 6–11.

need is not met, the existence of someone who could meet the need and do so at little cost to him or herself, and so on.

Needs are also relative to circumstance, although some needs – for example, the need for water – are relative to unalterable and/or invariable circumstances while some others, such as the need for a dentist, are not. Finally, some, but by no means all, needs generate moral rights and obligations. Suppose A has need for food and water but is unable to provide for these needs. If so, perhaps A has a right that B provide A with food and water if B is able to do so at little cost to B. On the other hand, if A has a need for friendship, it is far from clear that A has a right to B's friendship, even supposing that B could provide it at little cost to B.

It is generally accepted that an individual should help others – at least where she is the only one able to do so, the harm facing those others is serious and imminent, and the cost of providing assistance is relatively small. The same holds true of groups: there are collective responsibilities on the part of members of societies to assist one another, salient sub-groups. More generally, those who happen to be particularly well-placed to assist have collective responsibilities, whether or not they themselves belong to the needy group. Consider the following scenario. A group of bushwalkers comes across another bushwalker who has fallen and broken his leg. Without assistance, the bushwalker will die of exposure. No single member of the group could carry the injured person to safety, but if they act jointly they can do so without risk to themselves, or indeed any great inconvenience. It seems that, given their awareness of the near certainty of the death of the injured bushwalker if they do not intervene, the members of the group have a collective moral responsibility to take action.

So the need of groups for various forms of assistance that can only be adequately rendered by other groups generates collective responsibilities on the part of groups that can assist to do so.[13] Moreover, in our view, such responsibilities exist even where the harm is prospective rather than imminent. Of course, in many cases, the fact that a potential harm to others is temporally distant is relevant to whether or not we are the ones who have a duty to assist them in avoiding it, since there will be time for others who are better equipped to assist or can do so at a lower cost to intervene. But we can see no reason for holding that whether or not we have a duty to assist can depend on the temporal proximity of the harm, in itself.

Where such collective responsibilities to assist can most effectively be discharged by establishing institutions and institutional roles whose institutional duties consist of providing such aid, such as doctors and hospitals, then members

---

13 Miller, S., *Social Action: A Teleological Account*, New York: Cambridge University Press, 2001, Chapter 8; Miller, S., *The Moral Foundations of Social Institutions: A Philosophical Study*, New York: Cambridge University Press, 2009, Chapter 4. See also Alexandra, A., and Miller, S., 'Ethical Theory, "Common Morality" and Professional Obligations', *Theoretical Medicine and Bioethics*, vol. 30, no. 1, 2009, pp. 69–80 in which an earlier version of the material in this section appeared.

of the group who have the collective responsibility have a derivative responsibility to establish and support such institutions.

Further, members of a given group may have collective moral responsibilities towards the membership of that very group, that is, the group of which they are members. Assume that there is a high probability of a disease, say tuberculosis, taking the lives of some very small percentage of Australia's population, but that with respect to any individual Australian the risk is close to zero. In this situation, all or most Australians have a collective moral responsibility to prevent TB, and that responsibility can be discharged at minimal cost and inconvenience to any individual Australian. However, from the perspective of narrow individual self-interest, each Australian would not contribute. In the first place, given the almost zero possibility of harm to his or her self-interest, each does not have an incentive to contribute to the prevention of TB. And in the second place, even if such a cooperative scheme existed, self-interest would dictate that each putative participant free-ride. We conclude that the health care provision in question is undertaken in large part as a consequence of a perceived collective moral responsibility, and might initially take the form of local volunteer health care services. In due course, a division of labour tends to evolve, and the institution of professional medical practitioners is established to discharge the collective moral responsibility to avoid the harms caused by diseases such as TB.

The (collective) duty to assist may, then, in certain cases, imply the duty to establish and support institutions to achieve the object of the duty. Once such institutions with their specialized role holders are in place it may be that we generally have no further duty to assist within the area of the institutions' operations. Indeed, it may be that, generally, we should not even *try* to assist, given our relative lack of expertise and the likelihood that we will get in the way of the role holders. Still, on occasions when no role holder is available to assist and we possess relevant capacities etc. the individual or collective duty becomes re-animated. Moreover, we may have an ongoing duty to ensure that these institutions remain in place.

Once institutions and their constitutive roles have been established on some adequate moral basis, such as the duty to aid, then those who undertake these roles necessarily put themselves under obligations of various kinds – obligations that attach to, and are in part constitutive of, those roles. To understand the specific content of professional role morality, then, we need to examine the purposes – to meet the aggregated health care needs, in the case of the health care professions – which the various professions have been formed to serve, and the way in which professional roles must be constructed in order to achieve those purposes. Of course, one only comes to have a professional role through voluntary action, but the morality that comes with that role is not itself ultimately grounded on the individual's choice.

Everyone has a general duty to assist. We have provided an account of the moral basis of the medical profession, and its associated role morality, in particular, grounded on that duty. This account has two parts. First, an aggregate need – for example, for health care for Australians sufferers of TB – generates a collective responsibility on the part of Australians to put institutional arrangements in place that meet this need. Second, these arrangements comprise the institutional roles of doctor, nurse and the like, each with their constitutive professional rights and duties. These latter professional rights and duties are actually institutional specifications and instantiations of the underlying collective responsibility to the needy.

It is easy to see how this account can be generalized to other professions and other occupations that satisfy aggregated needs, or otherwise provide ethically required collective goods, in relation to which there is a collective moral responsibility.

Professional Autonomy and Self-regulation

Earlier we claimed that professional autonomy is a defining feature of the professions. The autonomy of members of the professions is no doubt an intrinsic good; after all, individual autonomy, more generally, is an intrinsic good. However, professional autonomy is not quite the same thing as individual autonomy, and it needs special justification.[14]

Professional autonomy concerns decision-making within the sphere of the professional role in question. As such, it is both narrower and wider than that of individual autonomy that pertains to areas outside the professional role. Moreover, since professional autonomy is an institutional right, it is not possessed purely by virtue of properties one possesses as a human being, albeit it is obviously in part derivative from individual human autonomy.

A professional exercises professional autonomy in this sense (and is possessed of the corresponding kind of institutional authority) when his or her decisions and actions in relation to the professional matters at issue are 'his or her call', that is, he or she is the one to make the decision, and his or her decision cannot be overridden by a superior. A surgeon, for example, has to make a decision as to whether to operate, a decision that cannot be overridden by a hospital administrator.

Contrast this kind of authority with that possessed by, say, a personnel officer. The personnel officer may be given only very general instructions about hiring policy and may exercise a good deal of discretion in the choices she actually makes. Nevertheless, her authority to employ new staff is delegated from a superior, who retains the right to withdraw it, and the right to overrule it in particular cases.

---

14 An earlier version of the material in this section is to be found in Alexandra, A., Campbell, T., Cocking, D., Miller, S., and White, K., *Professionalisation, Ethics and Integrity: The Promotion of Professional Ethical Standards and the Protection of Clients and Customers*, Report for the Professional Standards Council, 2006, pp. 1–185. On the notion of autonomy see also Miller, S., 'Individual Autonomy and Sociality', in F. Schmitt (ed.), *Socialising Metaphysics: Nature of Social Reality*, Lanham: Rowman & Littlefield, 2003, pp. 269–300. On the notion of professional autonomy see Miller, S., and Blackler, J., *Ethical Issues in Policing*, Aldershot: Ashgate, 2005, Chapter 2.

Professional autonomy tends to go hand in glove with professional liability. Thus, the surgeon, and not necessarily the hospital, is the one to be sued if the surgeon makes a mistake. This is how it should be. If the surgeon is to be the one who makes the decision then, rationally and morally, he ought to be the one who is held liable, if the decision is a bad one. Conversely, if the surgeon is to be held liable, then surely he must be the one given the right to make the decision.

We need to distinguish the autonomy of an individual institutional actor from institutional autonomy, i.e. the autonomy of the institution (or its leadership) vis-à-vis other institutions. In the case of professionals, the relevant institution would be the professional body, e.g. the Law Society.

We should also distinguish between autonomy and independence. Independence is a necessary condition for autonomy; if one is subject to external control one is not independent and to that extent one lacks autonomy. However, independence is not a sufficient condition for autonomy, since one could be independent of external control but lack self-mastery. Consider, for example, an unsupervised child; the child is independent but, since it lacks self-mastery, it is not autonomous.

The ultimate justification for professional autonomy – as opposed to individual autonomy per se – is provided by the (collective) ends of the professional role in question. Thus, surgeons ought to have professional autonomy just because this is the best way to maximize the health of patients, given the expertise and knowledge possessed by surgeons (but not by non-surgeons).

We have argued that the professions have a number of distinctive features that mark them off from other occupations. It must also be said that, in recent times, a number of the professions, notably lawyers and accountants, have come into disrepute, in part as a consequence of their role in corporate scandals, such as Enron and the collapse of Arthur Andersen. Increasingly, accountants and solicitors, for example, are housed in large corporations and, as a consequence, subjected to commercial pressures of a kind that can compromise their professional integrity.

Let us turn directly to the issue of the regulation of professional groups, given that members of these groups are, and ought to be, possessed of a degree of professional autonomy.

Historically, the paradigmatic professions have enjoyed a good deal of independence, at both the collective and individual level. This independence has been in large part manifest in their being allowed as a collective to self-regulate in relation to the setting, and enforcing the standards and norms of professional conduct; this is *professional self-regulation*. In addition, individual professional practitioners have enjoyed considerable autonomy in the application of those standards and norms in professional work; this is *individual professional autonomy*.

Prior to the question of whether professionals should self-regulate, there is the question of whether they should be regulated at all, beyond the minimal regulation of any market necessary to ensure respect for the 'rules of the game', such as prohibitions on the use of force and fraud, and enforcement of contracts. In ordinary markets, anyone can compete to provide goods or services that are attractive to consumers, who in turn can freely choose from those goods on offer. The needs-based account of professional work outlined above indicates the ways in which markets in professional services differ from markets in ordinary goods, and implies that, at least in some cases, professional work does require further regulation. The client has a need which they look to the professional to provide, but they may not know exactly what it is that they need, or what is the best means to its provision (think of a person with stomach pains going to a doctor, for example). This means that many clients are vulnerable to incompetence, exploitation and so on at the hands of professionals. Moreover, given the seriousness of the needs which many clients have, any failure to satisfy them may have very serious, perhaps irreversible, consequences. Regulation of professionals seems justified, then, at least to the extent to which it protects consumers from these risks, and makes it more likely that professionals will act in ways that are conducive to the realization of their defining end.

These sorts of considerations were in fact influential in the drive to ensure that those who offered these kinds of services were certified as competent to do so, and licensed to practice.[15] Such licensing serves two purposes. First, it provides assurance to the consumer that the service provider is able, and willing, to provide the service to a satisfactory standard. Secondly, at least if there is a realistic chance of losing certification for incompetence or wrongdoing, it provides an incentive for the professional to try to ensure that they do provide satisfactory service – which in turn underpins the consumer's assurance.

Professional regulation can thus be seen as having two major parts: admission to the profession; and regulation of the conduct of those admitted.[16] This second part, regulation of conduct, in turn involves setting and applying norms; and reporting and responding to violations of norms. Professional norms[17] can be classified into three broad categories. First, each profession develops *technical norms* governing the application of professional technical expertise in practice. For example, before prescribing medication to a patient, doctors should inquire whether the patient is taking other medication, and know if the medication they wish to prescribe is

15 See Carr-Saunders, A.M., and Wilson, P.A., *The Professions*, Oxford: Clarendon Press, 1933.

16 Bayles, M.D., 'Professional Power and Self-Regulation', *Business and Professional Ethics Journal*, vol. 5, no. 2, 1986, pp. 26–46.

17 A norm, in the sense in which we use it here, is in the first instance a prescriptive concept – it refers to a standard that members of a group believe should govern their behaviour, and which they are prepared to publicly espouse and defend. So understood, there can be significant divergences between, on the one hand, the actual behaviour of the group and the expectations they have of each other, and on the other the norms they espouse. Confidentiality and respect for clients might be norms for a group, even though many of them gossip about their clients and ridicule them behind their backs. Nevertheless, a norm must have some action guiding force. In the case mentioned, for example, the norm will still hold if members of the group will not engage in such behaviour in public, feel ashamed if it is brought to light, accept sanctions for violating it, and so on.

counter-indicated for the medication already being used; architects should have their designs tested for stability; and so on. Secondly, professions develop *ethical norms*: doctors, social workers and other human service professionals have strong obligations of confidentiality; there is a very strong prohibition on counsellors having sexual relations with their clients; and so on. Finally, professions often develop *economic norms* governing matters such as whether and how members are allowed to advertise their services, restrictions on over- (or under-) charging clients, and so on.[18]

We can now turn to the question of who should be involved in deciding what these various norms should be, and how they should be applied. Here we point to some general considerations that are relevant to the question of who should make decisions. Reasons in favour of giving someone decision-making power include the following:

- *Possession of expertise* – if someone has special expertise relevant to a decision, this is a reason to involve them in making it.
- *Bearing the consequences* – if a person is going to bear the consequences of a decision, that is a good reason for them to make it. There is both a pragmatic and a moral justification for this principle. Pragmatically, people are likely to be motivated to take more care over decisions that are likely to affect their own interests. Morally, the principle reflects the value of autonomy. To make decisions that will significantly affect other people without allowing them to influence that decision demonstrates a lack of respect for their status as autonomous beings.

On the other hand, reasons for not giving people decision-making power include the following:

- *Incompetence* – if someone lacks relevant expertise or knowledge in some area, they are obviously less well-equipped to make a good decision.
- *Conflict of interest* – someone has a conflict of interest when their personal interest comes into conflict with their occupational duties, or when they have two occupational roles, and the duties of one compete with the duties of the other. (We discuss conflicts of interest in more detail in Chapter 5.) A

18 We reiterate that despite the terminology used to describe these norms they are all broadly, or at least potentially, ethical in nature, since they will be judged in the light of their contribution to the realization of the overarching aim of the profession, which itself is a moral good. Consider a case where it is suggested that members of a profession should enforce a minimum fee rate (an economic norm). If charging less than this rate makes it likely that practitioners will not have sufficient economic means to provide the minimal level of service necessary to satisfy the needs of their clients, then it is (morally) justified. If it is simply a device to reduce competition and increase the remuneration of members, it is not.

role bearer with a conflict of interest who is making a decision may not be able to exclude considerations that are, from the point of view of the role, irrelevant to that decision. Their decision is thus likely to be worse than if they did not have a conflict of interest.

While these are important factors for and against giving those to whom they apply decision-making power, this is not supposed to be an exhaustive list. Moreover, the various reasons can come into conflict: someone who has a high degree of relevant expertise may also have a conflict of interest; another person who will bear the consequences of a decision may be less than fully competent, and so on.

As well as these general considerations regarding the allocation of decision-making power, there are some considerations that are particular to professional groups. In the first section of this chapter, we noted that professional communities tend to be organized as networks within which goods such as technical knowledge and access to clients circulate. Reputation becomes very important for network members, in three different kinds of ways. (We discuss reputation in more detail in Chapter 5.) First, there is what might be called internal reputation – the standing of each member in the eyes of their fellows. Since high standing attracts prestige, referrals etc. then each member of the group has an incentive to promote his reputation among his peers. At the same time, each has an incentive to ensure that the reputation of others reflects their actual capability, behaviour etc. Second, there is the public reputation of each member – their reputation in the eyes of their potential clients and other interested parties. Third, there is the reputation of the network per se – is the group seen to possess and uphold high standards among its members? (Think, for example, of the current reputation of the auditing profession on the one hand, and the nursing profession on the other.) The reputation of the network per se is a kind of collective good[19] for members, since the public reputation of each member is likely to be influenced by it to a high degree. Publicity regarding bad (or good) behaviour of one member of the profession tends to affect the public standing not only of that person, but of all members of the network.

Reputational effects, therefore, generate incentives that pull in two different directions. It is in the interest of members of the profession to ensure that the internal reputation of each is as accurate as possible, since such a reputation will influence them in their own practice, helping them judge to whom they should look for expertise, to whom they should refer clients, and so on. On the other hand, it is also in the interests of members of a profession to ensure that the reputation of the profession per se is as high as possible, even if this is not an accurate reflection of the actual state of affairs. To this extent, they have an incentive not to respond to the bad behaviour of fellows in a way likely to draw it to public attention. They may ignore it, or they may deal with it through 'informal' sanctions, such

19 For an account of collective goods in the relevant sense see Miller, S., *The Moral Foundations of Social Institutions: A Philosophical Study*, New York: Cambridge University Press, 2009, Chapter 2.

as expressing their disapproval to the miscreant, stopping referring clients to them, and so on. Note too that the interest that members of the network have in each other are primarily technical and financial – they are often not affected one way or the other by members treating their clients unethically, unless that also involves, say, technical incompetence. So they may have no powerful reason (at least no powerful self-interested reason) to care about unethical behaviour of other members of the network towards their clients, and good reason to prefer that public knowledge of such behaviour be minimized.

As we pointed out above, professions are constituted in part by a professional community. The 'network effect' is in fact one of the ways in which this community perpetuates itself. Community identity – as an aspect of collegiality – is also fostered by working together, common education and ongoing professional training, as well as participation in professional bodies, and the socializing that goes with these activities. While we have pointed to the positive aspects of such collegiality, it can also have less desirable effects, encouraging a group solidarity resistant to outside control and scrutiny, and a toleration of inadequate performance.[20]

In the light of these various considerations, we turn now to a consideration of the suitability of professionals to make decisions regarding the setting and application of the various norms of professional behaviour. In all cases it would seem that professionals will bear the consequences of the setting and application of norms, so that is a reason to involve these professionals in deciding on the norms. But, of course, in many cases exactly the same applies to others, such as clients or members of the public.

Let us begin by considering what we have called technical norms. Members of a profession clearly possess specialized expertise directly relevant to the setting and application of such norms. What are the feasible methods for stabilizing the bank of a dam; were the unsuccessful efforts of an engineer to achieve this nevertheless reasonable in the circumstances? These are questions that engineers (for instance) seem particularly authoritatively placed to address – which is not to say that they should be the only ones involved.

We turn now to ethical norms. Given the role-relativity of what we have called the internal aspect of professional ethics, members of a profession can often claim a certain degree of relevant expertise regarding the ethical norms that apply to their profession. In virtue of their professional expertise, psychiatrists, for example, are presumably well-placed to judge how serious an impact on the therapeutic process

20 This has been a notorious problem, for example, in police forces. (See, for example, Miller, S., and Blackler, J., *Ethical Issues in Policing*, Aldershot: Ashgate, 2005, Chapter 5). Stephanie Mencimer discusses the difficulty in finding doctors to testify against other doctors in medical malpractice suits, a difficulty exacerbated by the willingness of medical associations to take aggressive action, including deregistration, against those who do testify, in 'The White Wall. A new code of conduct is taking hold of the medical profession: First do no harm—to your colleagues', at http://www.legalaffairs.org/issues/March-April-2004/story_mencimer_marpar04.msp (last accessed 17 March 2009).

a sexual relationship between a psychiatrist and their patient is likely to have, and thus whether there should or should not be a norm prohibiting it, and how stringent the norm should be. Similarly, professional expertise is relevant to judgements regarding the appropriate response to breaches of professional ethical norms. How much harm did this breach actually do, how wilful was the offender's disregard of the signs that harm was occurring?

On the other hand, there is no reason to think that members of a profession have greater expertise than anyone else regarding the external ethical aspects of professional practice. Furthermore, professionals and their clients may collude in unethical behaviour (such as an illicit sexual liaison) which is welcomed by both parties. In effect, these are 'victimless crimes', with attendant difficulties of detection and suppression. (Of course, this is far from the case for all ethical breaches – often clients are severely damaged by the unethical behaviour of professionals and are keen to report it.) Moreover, as discussed above, it is in the interest of professionals to protect the reputation of their profession per se, so there is a tendency for them not to seek out breaches of professional norms or fail to respond adequately to those which do come to their notice (this is in fact a kind of conflict of interest), a tendency that may be reinforced by collegial norms.

Finally, we consider economic norms. There may be good reason to have occupation-specific economic norms. Consider, for example, the imposition of the requirement that architects be guaranteed a fee that is not less than a certain percentage of the built cost of a structure designed by an architect. This can be rationalized as follows. If there is no minimum fee, architects will attempt to underbid each other to gain commissions. In many cases, the successful tenderer will only be able to obtain a reasonable financial return if they provide an 'off the shelf' design, with little attention given to site- or use-specific needs. While the cost to the developer will be less than it would have been if they had had to pay a set fee to the architect, the total cost of the building to its owners over its lifetime will be greater than if the architect had been able to spend more time and care in its design (because, for example it will require more heating and cooling), and the amenity to its users less. Hence, there are economic and social reasons to enforce minimum fee requirements.[21] Given their technical expertise, members of a profession may be able to provide information relevant to decisions concerning the setting of economic norms.

Generally, however, professionals do not possess any special economic expertise regarding the setting of such norms. Economic policy decisions usually involve cost-benefit analyses, where the costs and benefits at issue are wider than simple financial values. The weighing and calculation of costs relative to benefits of the various available courses of action does not usually fall into the domain of expertise of the professionals involved. Furthermore, even where the imposition of restrictive economic norms is justified, placing power in this area

21 Our aim here is not to adjudicate on whether or not fee-setting is justified in such cases. Our point is that professional expertise is relevant to that adjudication.

in a profession's hands generates an inherent conflict of interest – and history has shown that such power is often abused.[22] On the other hand, self-interest may also drive professionals to report and act on the economic misconduct of other members of the profession.

Our discussion supports the view that professionals should be involved in setting and enforcing the standards and norms of professional conduct. It does not support the claim that the professions should be entirely self-regulating, where 'self-regulation' is understood as a profession (or other body) agreeing to abide by voluntarily adopted standards embodied, for example, in a code of conduct or code of ethics. In a true self-regulating system, the relevant body has sole responsibility for regulating the conduct of its members. Neither the standards of conduct, nor the sanctions imposed are legislatively under-pinned, and the government does not directly intervene by monitoring behaviour, or applying sanctions. Given the problems of conflict of interest, and lack of expertise we have pointed to, and the effects of professionals on other groups, the case for self-regulation is weak. Generally, what seems to be called for is some form of 'co-regulation', where the state delegates regulatory powers to professional (or other occupational) groups, provided that they meet conditions such as developing and promulgating a code of ethics, establishing an effective complaints and discipline mechanism, requiring members to engage in ongoing professional education activities, and providing regular reports to an oversight body on these matters, demonstrating their effects in improving practice. On the one hand, given the requirement for the oversight body to be shown that regulation is actually effective, it overcomes the problems inherent in a pure system of self-regulation discussed above. On the other hand, it leaves the design and implementation of the regulatory system to those who are best placed to understand the ethical issues faced by members of the occupation and the way regulation actually impacts on them. (It follows that a well-designed co-regulatory system will ensure that all relevant stakeholders have input.)

---

22 See, for example, Lamont, J., 'The Ethics of Doctor Supply Restriction in Australia', *Australian Journal of Professional and Applied Ethics*, vol. 2, no. 2, 2001, pp. 10–19.

Chapter 2
Holistic Integrity Systems

Integrity Systems

Integrity systems can be contrasted with regulatory frameworks. A regulatory framework is a structured set of explicit laws, rules or regulations governing behaviour, issued by some institutional authority and backed by sanctions. It may serve to ensure compliance with minimum ethical standards (namely those embodied in a law, rule or regulation), but this is only one of its purposes. There are numerous laws, rules and regulations that have little or nothing to do with ethics. An integrity system, by contrast, is an assemblage of institutional entities, mechanisms and procedures, the purpose (collective end) of which is to ensure compliance with minimum *ethical* standards and promote the pursuit of *ethical* ideals.

Integrity systems for the profession will need to go beyond the ethical norms and ideals of good commercial practice. Specifically, they will need to address the requirement that the professions are realizing their defining collective end, i.e. serving the ends of justice, good health, and the like. Moreover, they will also need to ensure that professional rights are protected, professional duties discharged and professional virtues exercised. For example, an adequate integrity system will protect professional autonomy while ensuring professional accountability (see Chapter 1).

However, we need to be clearer about integrity systems.[1] The term, 'integrity system', has recently come into vogue in relation to what is, in fact, a very ancient problem for organizations, occupational groups and, indeed, whole polities and communities, namely the problem of promoting ethical behaviour and eliminating or reducing unethical behaviour.

Here, the term, 'system', is somewhat misleading in that it implies a clear and distinct set of integrated institutional mechanisms operating in unison and in accordance with determinate mechanical, or at least quasi-mechanical, principles. However, in practice, integrity 'systems' are a messy assemblage of formal and informal devices and processes, and they operate in often indeterminate, unpredictable and sometimes even conflicting ways.

---

1 See Miller, S., Roberts, P., and Spence, E., *Corruption and Anti-Corruption*, Saddle River, NJ: Prentice Hall, 2005, Chapter 7; and Miller, S., *The Moral Foundations of Social Institutions: A Philosophical Study*, New York: Cambridge University Press, 2009, Chapter 5.

The term, 'integrity', as used in the expression 'integrity system', is also problematic in that it appropriates a moral notion normally used to describe individual human agents, and applies it to organizations and other large groups of individuals. Roughly speaking, individual human persons have integrity if: (i) they possess the full array of central moral virtues, such as honesty, loyalty, and trustworthiness, and (ii) they exercise rational and morally informed judgement in their adherence to any given virtue, including when the requirements of different virtues might seem to come into conflict.

For example, persons with integrity would not allow themselves to act dishonestly out of a misplaced sense of loyalty, notwithstanding the importance of loyalty as one of the virtues possessed by a person with integrity.

By contrast with the notion of an individual person's integrity, integrity used in the context we are employing it here of an integrity system for a profession applies to the representative bodies, (e.g. American Medical Association), and oversight bodies, (e.g. the Office of the Legal Services Commissioner in Australia) of the particular group. It also applies to the large set of individual role occupants within the profession and the organizations for which they work, (e.g. hospitals, legal firms), as well as to the structure, function and culture of the group and its associated organizations, i.e. to the profession as a social institution.

The integrity of a profession is in large part dependent on the individual integrity of its members, and therefore an integrity system is in large part focused on developing and maintaining the individual integrity of these members. Nevertheless, these groups are not simply the sum of its members, and so determining the integrity levels for these groups is not simply a matter of summing the levels of integrity of the individuals who happen to be its members.

In the first place, the individuals who comprise professions are role occupants, and the responsibilities and virtues required of them are somewhat different from, and in some respects greater than, those required of ordinary individual persons not occupying such roles. So, for instance, scrupulous attention to numerical detail might be a constitutive virtue of the role of an accountant but not of the role of a husband. And, of course, the technical competencies for which the lawyer, medical doctor or engineer are responsible are not typically required of ordinary individual persons not occupying such roles.

Moreover, what counts as a professional responsibility or virtue, both in terms of technical and ethical competencies, varies greatly across different professional groups. The technical competencies for which the lawyer, medical doctor or engineer are each responsible are not common *across* these groups. Similarly, the virtues are often role specific.

While, arguably, the 'zealous advocacy of one's client's interests' might be a critical virtue to the role of a lawyer or barrister in adversarial legal systems, it is clearly not a critical virtue for the engineer. So what counts as integrity in an individual professional role occupant is neither captured by what counts as integrity in an ordinary person or what counts as integrity in some other occupational role. One important task then, for specific professional areas is to determine what precisely the constitutive virtues of the individual role-occupant are, and devise strategies to ensure that these virtues are developed and maintained in the members of that occupational or associational area.

In the second place, the integrity of a profession is not simply a matter of the integrity of the individual role occupants who comprise it, for the integrity of a profession is partly a matter of the structure, function and culture of the profession *qua* institution. Consider structure, both legal and administrative. In a profession possessed of integrity, the administrative processes and procedures in relation to, for example, promotion or complaints and discipline, would embody relevant ethical principles of fairness, procedural justice, transparency, and the like.

Now consider function (collective ends). In a profession possessed of integrity, the organizational goals actually being pursued would align closely with the collective ends, i.e. collective goods, of the profession, such as, for example, the promotion of public safety for engineers or of human health for doctors, rather than purely commercial guidance. Finally, consider culture. In a profession possessed of integrity, the pervasive ethos, or spirit, i.e. the culture, would be one that was, for example, conducive to high performance, both technically and ethically, and supportive in times of need, but intolerant of serious incompetence or misconduct.

In looking at options to promote integrity and combat ethico-professional failures it is very easy to leap to a particular single 'magic bullet' solution, such as increasing penalties or giving more intrusive powers to investigative agencies, and doing so without considering the full array of implications, including the demonstrable (as opposed to hoped for) benefits (which of these measures has been tested and, as a consequence, is *known* to work?), and the costs in terms of resources, damage to ethico-professional ethos, and so on.

Moreover, 'magic bullet' solutions are often offered in relative ignorance of both the actual nature and causes of the problems they are supposed to address. The truth is often in the detail.

So, for instance, many professions stand accused of being too tolerant of cases of serious incompetence or corruption and of being so for self-interested reasons of protecting professional reputation. Moreover, these self-interested reasons come at the expense of the legitimate interests of consumers or the public. No doubt there are cases in which serious incompetence or misconduct is tolerated at some cost to the legitimate interests of the consumer or the public. However, such tolerance need not arise because of reputational self-interested concerns.

There are at least two other significant factors commonly in play: namely, the difficulty of making judgements in some cases, especially 'unique' cases and, secondly, the highly litigious nature of the area. Unless, therefore, the nature of the problems, in particular their causes, are first identified there is little hope of finding a solution to such problems.

Moreover, in attempting to determine the causes of unethical professional practices there are a number of preliminary questions that need to be addressed. One set of questions pertains to the precise nature of the unethical practice at issue, and the context in which it occurs. What is the motivation? Are there, for example, as above, some compelling practical facts that explain the practice? What other pressures and opportunities might there be for the unethical practice in question? Another set of questions concerns the extent of the corruption or unethical practice: is it sporadic or continuing, restricted to a few 'rotten apples' or widespread within the area? Here, as elsewhere, rhetoric is no substitute for evidence-based conclusions.

Even when the answers to these questions have been provided there will arise further questions in relation to any remedies proposed. For example, any contemplation of mechanisms to redress ethico-professional misconduct that will require the expenditure of energy and resources – and may well impinge on individual freedom – needs to be justified in terms of the seriousness and extent of the misconduct to be successfully combated.

Second, and more importantly, understanding the causes of ethico-professional misconduct and failures and the tailoring of remedies to address them will involve considering and distinguishing between three sorts of motivation for compliance with moral principles.

One reason for compliance is the fear of punishment; hence the use, or threatened use, of the so-called big stick. So, for instance, agent A does not steal from agent B because A fears she will get caught and locked up. A second reason for compliance arises from the benefit to oneself. Hence the possible utility of the so-called carrot approach. So, for instance, B pays B's workers reasonable wages because by doing so the workers are healthy, work productively, and B makes good profits. These two reasons are essentially appeals to self-interest. Taken in combination they constitute the 'stick-carrot' approach much loved by many contemporary economists. However, there is a third reason for compliance. This is the moral belief or desire to do what is right. A refrains from stealing because A believes that it is morally wrong to steal; B pays B's workers reasonable wages because B desires to be fair.

Here, we need first to note the contrast between appeals to moral beliefs and appeals to self-interest. Acting from a concern to do what is right or good does not turn on whether or not it is in one's self-interest. It may or may not be in one's own self-interest to, say, be honest or fair. Moreover, the notion of persons acting out of moral rectitude is completely at odds with the essentially manipulative approach of those who advocate *only* sticks and carrots.

That said however, there are also important connections to be highlighted and promoted between self-interest and morality so that these conceptions are more in balance and integrated and less at odds. First, of course, the appeal to morality must be balanced by the appeal to self-interest. If, for instance, it is at great cost to self to be, say honest or fair, then one may have sufficient reason to not be honest or fair. Indeed, the reason need not be purely self-interested but also count as moral. So, for instance, if my family and my livelihood are threatened, then I may have significant reasons from both prudence and morality to, say, steal.

It is evident that widespread and ongoing compliance typically requires appeals to self-interest (sticks and carrots) but also appeals to moral beliefs. Ideally, integrity systems should have penalties for those who do not comply, should enable benefits to flow to those who do comply, and should resonate with the moral beliefs of the people thus regulated; for instance, laws and regulations should be widely thought to be just.

Therefore, institutional design that proceeds on the assumption that self-interest is the only human motivation worth considering fails. It fails because it overlooks the centrality of moral beliefs in human life, and therefore does not mobilize moral sentiment. On the other hand, institutional design that proceeds on the assumption that self-interest can be ignored, and that a sense of moral duty on its own will suffice, also fails; it fails because self-interest is an ineradicable and pervasive feature of all human groups. In this connection, we note the importance of reputation to self-interest; reputational loss can have a devastating impact on members of the profession, notably in financial terms. In Chapter 5 we provide a detailed discussion of reputation and the role that the mobilization of reputation can play in enhancing integrity systems.

Reactive Integrity Systems

Integrity systems can be thought of as being either predominantly reactive or predominantly preventive.[2] Naturally, the distinction is somewhat artificial, since there is a need for both reactive elements, e.g., a complaints and discipline system, as well as preventive elements, e.g. ethics training and transparency of processes, in any adequate integrity system. At any rate, integrity systems can be considered under the two broad headings, reactive and preventive.

The reactive way of dealing with ethico-professional misconduct and corruption is the one that first comes to mind. The logic is direct: the activity is defined as one that is not acceptable; an individual engages in that activity and therefore, as a direct result, should be held to account for the misconduct and, if found guilty, disciplined in some way. The rationale for the reactive response for dealing with unethical behaviour, including criminality and corruption, is threefold: offenders are held to account for their actions; offenders get their just deserts; and potential offenders are deterred from future offences.

Reactive mechanisms for dealing with unethical behaviour are fundamentally linear: setting out a series of offences (usually in legislation or regulations), waiting for an individual to transgress, then investigating, adjudicating, and finally taking punitive action. Complaints and discipline systems are basically reactive institutional mechanisms. Naturally, these systems are also preventative mechanisms by virtue

2 An earlier version of the material in this section and the following two sections appeared in Miller, S., Roberts, P., and Spence, E., *Corruption and Anti-Corruption*, Saddle River, NJ: Prentice Hall, 2005, Chapter 7.

of their deterrence role; however, the adequacy of this deterrence role is typically dependent on their effectiveness qua reactive mechanisms, i.e. their success in detecting, investigating and prosecuting offenders.

Reactive integrity mechanisms are a necessary part of any feasible integrity system. Sometimes, however, too much reliance is placed on them, and the weaknesses of the reactive approach are made manifest.

One obvious weakness is the passivity of the approach; by the time the investigators swing into action, the damage has been already done. Another problem stems from the fact that unethical behaviour is often secretive, e.g. professional associations may 'close ranks' to protect the reputation of the group.

A further problem stems from the inadequacy of the resources to investigate and successfully prosecute; investigation and prosecution is resource intensive. Consider fraud in this connection. Fraud is widespread in modern economies, yet police and other agencies simply do not have the resources to investigate adequately all the reports of fraud brought to their attention. Consequently, if the chances of being caught or complained about are relatively slight due to under-resourcing, the deterrent effect is undermined, which in turn means there is an even larger number of offences and offenders for investigators to deal with.

Of course, the effectiveness of a reactive approach requires that significant detection mechanisms are available. Those who engage in ethico-professional misconduct then have at least two good reasons to fear exposure: first, detection may lead to legal or associational sanctions, such as fines, suspension or expulsion from the industry, and, second, it may lead to moral sanctions emanating from work colleagues, community, and from significant others, e.g., friends and relatives. Nevertheless, there are a number of sources of information in relation to most forms of ethico-professional misconduct and corruption. One of the most important is fellow-workers who may report such conduct or suspicious activity to superiors, or even blow the whistle.

Having considered the general nature of the reactive approach to dealing with ethical misconduct, it is now necessary to examine two central planks of the linear and logical progression that proceed from the offences that are set down in legislation and in regulations, move to the detection of the offence and its investigation, and finally to prosecution and the imposition of punishment – namely, the legal framework and the investigative process. It is clear that ethical misconduct embraces a wide variety of activities, ranging from serious criminal offences, e.g. fraud, through to non-criminal professional misconduct that may warrant disciplinary measures, e.g. conflict of interest, and on to minor ethical infringements, e.g. rudeness, which might call for counselling or the like. For the purposes of this analysis, we will concentrate upon ethical misconduct that is identified in criminal codes and is subject to criminal investigation processes; we do so on the understanding that the criminal justice system represents the most salient and sophisticated, reactive institutional response to combating serious forms of unethical behaviour. Note that in Chapter 4 we provide a detailed treatment of complaints and discipline systems and, therefore, of the reactive response to non-criminal ethical misconduct.

Legislative and Regulatory Frameworks

Almost every jurisdiction has criminal laws against self-evident forms of serious ethical misconduct by members of occupational groups in occupational settings, for example fraud, theft, offering or soliciting bribes, or abusing the power of a public office.

While it is common for anti-corruption laws and other criminal laws to be consolidated into a criminal code, it is almost universal that legislation dealing with particular areas of activity, such as the regulation of companies and corporations, will also contain criminal offence provisions. In essence, these provisions will be dealing with the same issues of abuse of office, bribery, theft, fraud and so on, but in a more specific context.

At the core of dealing with serious ethical misconduct using reactive mechanisms is the codification of the community's moral attitudes into statutes, regulations, or other such instruments. These are enacted by a legislature and embody a fragment of the basic social norms of the community. By virtue of embodying social norms in a community, anti-corruption laws and the like reflect the moral beliefs of the community; by virtue of being laws passed by the duly elected representatives of the community, criminal law reflects the will of the community.

The creation and maintenance of a legislative regime to deal with serious ethical misconduct involves a number of difficulties. As the current international financial crisis has served to underline yet again, in the sphere of commercial activity there is an ever-present financial incentive to find ways to avoid compliance with laws and regulations. As a consequence, there is a constant need to monitor compliance with the regulatory system in order either to ensure that new forms of corruption have not been found, or, if they have, to enable legislative changes to be made to defeat them. This is presumably so in the case of the so-called toxic financial products that constitute part of the current problems, i.e. non-transparent packaged bundles of mortgages (including sub-prime mortgages) incorrectly assessed by ratings agencies as high quality on the spurious grounds that the investment banks that packaged them allegedly had good risk assessment processes. Given its infamy and the availability of detailed analyses, consider the case of Enron. Here, an array of techniques was used to undermine the regulatory framework existing at that time, including so-called Special Purpose Entities (SPEs).

SPEs, which were a specialty of Andrew Fastow (Enron's Chief Financial Officer), were initially introduced by banks and law firms as 'structured finance' – complex financial deals intended to enable companies to generate tax deductions and move assets off a company's books.[3] With names such as Cactus, Braveheart,

3 See Behr, P., and Witt, A. (*Washington Post* Staff Writers), 'Visionary's Dream Led to Risky Business', *Washington Post*, 28 July, 2002.

Whitewing, JEDI, Chewco, Raptors, LJM I and LJM II (named after Fastow's wife Lea and his two children), Enron used SPEs for various purposes. The primary purpose was for financing new projects in Enron's ever-expanding trading business, which continuously needed new injections of cash funds to sustain that expansion, as well as providing insurance hedging for those projects whilst managing – sometimes legally, but mostly not – to keep debt related to those projects off its balance sheet, whilst taking up earnings relating to those projects in its income statements. For his role in those SPEs, Andrew Fastow reportedly made more than US$45 million. In the wake of the revelations concerning Fastow's key role in the Enron SPEs, especially Chewco and LJM – and just one month prior to Enron's final collapse and bankruptcy on 2 December 2001 – the company was forced to restate its earnings from 1997 through to 2002, which required a US$1.2 billion equity write-down.

The Enron collapse and the damage wrought on the international financial system by toxic financial products have highlighted the difficulty that legislatures face in establishing and maintaining a regulatory regime in such complex and rapidly changing fields.

Investigation

In order to bring serious offenders to justice, there needs to be an investigative capacity. Most typically this is the police service, but large organizations typically have their own investigative units, e.g. ethics and fraud units, and in many jurisdictions bodies with the specific responsibility to deal with corruption have been established. Investigators need to be specifically trained, have powers to question witnesses, and prepare evidence for prosecution.

On the one hand, these investigators are, as already noted, in a difficult position by virtue of being under-resourced agencies confronting often well-resourced individuals and corporate organizations. Moreover, in the case of investigators employed by large corporations, in particular, there can be issues of investigative independence; to what extent is investigative independence compromised, for example, when the subject of their investigation is a very senior person within the organization that employs them?

On the other hand, investigators and the agencies they work for are often in a very powerful position. They have access to an enormous amount of personal information, which could potentially be used to violate the privacy of employees and citizens. Moreover, by virtue of their crucial role in the effective handling of serious unethical conduct, these individuals are subject to significant pressures to engage in unethical conduct themselves. Accordingly, it is very important to have accountability mechanisms in relation to the investigators and their agencies. These mechanisms should have all the elements of a reactive system: offences set down in legislation, an independent authority to determine cases, powers to investigate, and specific penalties (like the loss of pension entitlements for investigators found to be corrupt).

Proceeding further along the linear process of reactive action, effective handling of serious ethical misconduct requires that detection mechanisms are available. Those engaged in serious ethical misconduct have at least two good reasons to fear exposure; first, detection may lead to criminal sanctions, and second, it may lead to moral sanctions emanating from the community and from significant others, e.g. friends and relatives. As we have seen above, there are a number of sources of information in relation to serious offenders. One of the most important is fellow workers, who may report corrupt or suspicious activity to superiors.

There are other sources of information in relation to serious ethical misconduct that investigators can use to assist them in their task. The advent of computers has seen the capacity to record and track virtually all financial transactions. Countries such as Australia have stringent and elaborate arrangements controlling the operation of accounts in financial institutions, and requirements for the reporting of cash transactions over a certain limit, identifying and reporting suspicious transactions, and monitoring all overseas money transactions. This provides an invaluable source of information that can be used to detect corruption, and assist in its prosecution. As is the case with many of the mechanisms for dealing with criminality, transaction analysis is a very beneficial tool, but it comes at a moral cost; it impinges upon the privacy of members of the community. This is because transaction analysis involves vast amounts of information on citizens' financial activities being recorded and transmitted to enforcement agencies.

Preventative Integrity Systems

A preventive integrity system will typically embrace, or act in tandem with, a reactive integrity system. However, we can consider preventive mechanisms for dealing with ethico-professional misconduct independent of any reactive elements. If we do so, we see that they can be divided into three categories.

- Institutional mechanisms for promoting an environment in which integrity is rewarded and, as a consequence, unethical behaviour is discouraged; this is an attempt to reduce the desire or motivation to act unethically, so that opportunities for unethical behaviour are not pursued or taken, even when they arise.
- The array of institutional mechanisms which limit (or eliminate) the opportunity for unethical behaviour. Such mechanisms include corporate governance mechanisms such as separating the roles of receiving accounts and paying accounts to reduce the opportunity for fraud.
- Those institutional mechanisms which act to expose unethical behaviour, so that the organization, or community can deal with them. The term 'transparency' may be used to characterize these mechanisms.

We accept that this threefold distinction is somewhat artificial, and that some institutional mechanisms will in fact come under more than one heading, and indeed that some, e.g. regulations, have both a reactive, as well as a preventive role.

The first category in our breakdown of prevention mechanisms are those institutional processes that exist to promote ethical behaviour. This category is made up of those components of an integrity system that engage with the individual's desire to do what is morally right and avoid what is morally wrong, and to be morally approved of by others for so acting. These institutional instruments include *codes of ethics* and *professional development programs.* We discuss codes of ethics in Chapter 3 and professional development programs in Chapter 6.

Reducing Opportunities for Unethical Behaviour

An important aspect of integrity systems is in the reduction of opportunities for individuals and organizations to engage in unethical behaviour. There are multifarious institutional mechanisms devised to reduce such opportunities, ranging from physical security (e.g. safes, locks and keys, computer passwords, firewalls), and personnel security (e.g. background checks, surveillance and monitoring of employees), through to role specifications (e.g. investigators not being subject to the authority of those they investigate), and the design of mechanisms to deal with known sources of ethical misconduct (e.g. conflicts of interest).

Some mechanisms in this regard are:

- Separation of financial functions, e.g. accounts payable divided from accounts receivable.
- Conflict of interest prohibitions for individuals, e.g. conflicting financial interests, outside employment activities (see Chapter 4).
- Elimination of structural conflicts of interest. For example, Arthur Andersen was Enron's auditor and yet earned US$52 million in fees in 2000 from Enron – indeed, Enron was Arthur Andersen's largest client, and Arthur Andersen acted as Enron's management consultant.
- 'Revolving door' restrictions on public officials leaving their positions to work for companies whose business it is to lobby governments, or that have significant business dealings with governments. The concern arises from the suspicion that prior to leaving, the officials will set up (in secret) highly lucrative deals so as to attract high salaries from their future employers, and/or use their extensive social contacts within government to give their new employer an unfair advantage.
- Eliminate excessive payments to management. Consider the recent widespread media reports in 2009 relating to huge payments to AIG executives.
- Limit executive stock options so as to reduce the interest executives might have in ignoring suspect deals that, if terminated, would negatively impact on the share price.

- Stringent accountability mechanisms to deal with power imbalances between superiors and subordinates in relation to, for example, promotion within an organization.
- Independent auditing; the knowledge that an independent body will be examining the financial records of an organization acts to inhibit unethical activity. For example, Enron staff deliberately ignored accepted accounting practice in the valuing of assets when they conspired with the banks to represent loans as profits.
- Tendering and contracting procedures, including requirements to advertise tenders, to ensure there is clear specification of the work to be done and of the criteria for success in the tender process, and also to have systems to guarantee that tenders are not accessed by persons other than the designated authorities.

Transparency

Let us now turn to the last of the three types of preventative mechanisms for dealing with serious unethical behaviour, namely transparency mechanisms.

One of the most important conditions conducive to corruption and many other forms of unethical behaviour is secretiveness. Hence, the importance of transparency mechanisms, i.e. mechanisms that ensure that transactions are conducted openly, and/or are subject to appropriate scrutiny.

At a national level, a fully functioning parliamentary system plays a central role in deterring ethical misconduct in the public sector; for public sector officials are required to go through a detailed and rigorous process in relation to their expenditure of public monies and their exercise of the powers vested in the public offices that they occupy. Congressional committees in the United States, and parliamentary committees in the United Kingdom and Australia, play a crucial role in making officials accountable for their actions by using powers to require those officials to explain their actions. At a less dramatic level, there are a variety of public institutions that operate to enable the community to be assured that officials are acting in accordance with the detailed accounting requirements that are in place in the public sector. One of these is the Auditor-General (or the General Accounting Office in the United States). Reports of these bodies make transparent the details of expenditure of public monies.

Operating at yet another level, are those mechanisms of transparency that enable citizens to access reasons for decisions that affect them (Administrative Appeals Tribunal Act, Administrative Decisions (Judicial Review) Act) and information (Freedom of Information Act, Privacy Act, Archives Act). All the mechanisms described above operate to open the workings of government to scrutiny and therefore enable the community to assess whether they are being governed in a way that meets their expectations of integrity.

A parallel, although typically less onerous, set of transparency mechanisms operate in the commercial sphere. Companies are required to file certain reports about their activities and these are made public. The intent behind these processes is to make key decisions transparent, and to assist the community in making judgments about investments. These transparency mechanisms have the force of law, and failure to comply with them is a criminal offence.

Before leaving the role of transparency, it is necessary to note the crucial role the media plays in the exposure of serous ethical misconduct, and, therefore, if the other mechanisms are operating effectively, in reducing unethical behaviour. A vibrant and free media is essential in bringing to the community's attention corruption and other serious forms of unethical behaviour – whether they occur in the corporate sector, like Enron, or in the public sector.

Holistic Integrity Systems

Thus far in the analysis of integrity systems, we have looked at integrity systems and mechanisms under the headings of reactive systems and preventive systems. It is evident that in most societies, jurisdictions, and indeed organizations, the attempt to combat unethical behaviour involves both reactive and preventive systems.

That is, integrity-building strategies involve reactive systems as well as preventive systems, and within preventive systems there are mechanisms that promote ethical behaviour, there are corporate governance mechanisms with, for example, anti-fraud or corruption functions, and there are various transparency mechanisms.

Moreover, it seems clear that an adequate integrity system cannot afford to do without reactive as well as preventive systems; and that preventive systems need to have all the elements detailed above. This suggests that there are two important issues. The first is the adequacy of each of the elements of the above systems, e.g. how adequate are the complaints and discipline processes, including the investigative capacity? Or how effective are the mechanisms of transparency? The second issue pertains to the level of integration and congruence between the reactive and the preventive systems; to what extent do they act together to mutually reinforce one another?

In this connection, it is worth noting that many jurisdictions have 'watchdog' agencies. Such bodies are established by statutes that also define a range of offences, have powers to investigate and refer matters to the courts for prosecution. However, it is notable that these watchdog agencies also involve themselves in prevention programs involving the development of preventive mechanisms; they no longer see their role as merely that of a reactive agency.

We should think of effective integrity systems, therefore, as holistic in character, and conceive of specific integrity building mechanisms as elements of a holistic integrity system. In looking at the set of integrity building processes as a holistic system, we need first to remind ourselves what is presupposed by an integrity system.

First, and most obviously, there must be some shared moral values in relation to the moral unacceptability of specific forms of behaviour, and a disapproval of those who engage in such behaviour. That is, there needs to be a framework of accepted social norms.

Second, there needs to be a broadly shared conception in relation to what needs to be done (the institutional means) to minimize it (the collective end); for example, should it be simply criminalized or should the response include restorative elements?

Third, there needs to be present some capacity to create and implement institutional mechanisms that deal with the issue of unethical behaviour and corruption, and this presumes some form of legal or regulatory system and organizational structure. Here, considerations of efficiency and effectiveness are important.

Finally, there needs to be some source of authority whereby sanctions can be applied to individuals who engage in unethical behaviour. However, this needs to be done in the context of an understanding that (and a holistic integrity system in which) reducing unethical behaviour is a *collective* moral responsibility. To this issue we now turn.

Collective Moral Responsibility and Integrity Systems

Collective moral responsibility is not the same thing as individual moral responsibility. Nevertheless, collective moral responsibility is to be understood in individualist terms.

An individualist account of collective moral responsibility ascribes moral responsibility only to individual human beings, as opposed to collective entities.[4] On this kind of view, collective entities, e.g. social groups and organizations, have collective moral responsibility only in the sense that the individual human persons who constitute such entities have individual moral responsibility, either individually or jointly.

We can usefully distinguish four senses of collective responsibility.

Two or more individuals perform a joint action if each of them intentionally performs an individual action, but does so with the true belief that in so doing they will jointly realize an end which each of them has. Having an end in this sense is a mental state of one or more individuals; it is an end that is not realized by one individual acting alone; it is a collective end. For example, you and I lifting a heavy box onto a truck is a joint action, since you lift one side and I lift the other, each of us lifts his side truly believing the other will lift theirs, and each of us has as an end – a collective end – that the box be situated on the truck.

4 Miller, S., 'Collective Moral Responsibility: An Individualist Account', in P.A. French (ed.), *Midwest Studies in Philosophy*, 2006, vol. XXX, pp. 176–193.

Agents who perform a joint action are responsible for that action in the first sense of collective responsibility, i.e. natural responsibility.

Each agent is individually (naturally) responsible for performing his contributory action, and is responsible by virtue of the fact that he intentionally performed this action, and the action was not intentionally performed by anyone else; the other agents (or agent) *believe* that he is performing, has performed, or is going to perform, the contributory action in question.

The agents are collectively or jointly responsible for the realization of the collective end; the realization of the collective end results from the performance of their contributory actions, e.g. two agents are collectively or jointly (naturally) responsible for bringing it about that the tendering process unfairly delivers the contract to the bribe-giver or that the bribery or fraudulent act is detected and those responsible brought to justice.

If the occupants of an institutional role (or roles) have an institutionally determined obligation to perform some joint action then those individuals are collectively responsible for its performance; this is collective *institutional* responsibility. There is a *joint* institutional obligation to realize the collective end; there is also a set of derived *individual* obligations, for example of the investigator to interview the suspects.

The third sense of collective responsibility is the responsibility of those in authority; this is a species of institutional responsibility. Thus, members of the cabinet of a parliament collectively decide to increase corporate taxes, and instruct the commissioner for taxation to implement this decision. The cabinet is collectively institutionally responsible for the tax increase by virtue of the fact that each of the members of the cabinet – jointly with the other members – agreed that there was to be a tax increase and these members jointly stand in an authority relation to the commissioner for taxation.

An agent is morally responsible for an action if the agent was naturally responsible for the action, i.e. the agent intentionally performed the action and did so for a reason, and the action was morally significant.

On the view being proffered, collective moral responsibility is a species of joint responsibility; each agent is individually morally responsible, but this is conditional on the others being individually morally responsible: there is interdependence in respect of moral responsibility.

Accordingly, we can derive the following principle: if agents are collectively responsible for the realization of an outcome, in the first, second or third senses of collective responsibility, and the outcome is morally significant, then – other things being equal – the agents are collectively *morally* responsible for that outcome, and can reasonably attract moral praise or blame, and (possibly) punishment or reward for bringing about the outcome.

In the case of a morally significant joint action, each agent is *individually* morally responsible for performing his *contributory* action, and the other agents are not morally responsible for his individual contributory action. In addition, however, the contributing agents are *collectively* morally responsible for the outcome or collective end.

Note that joint responsibility involves interdependence of responsibility, as opposed to interdependence of action. Each agent is individually morally responsible for realizing the relevant collective end, but conditionally on the others being individually morally responsible for realizing it.

There are some morally significant joint actions in which each of the participating agents makes a very small causal contribution and in which the collective end is an end only in an attenuated sense. In many of these cases, most participants have only a radically diminished moral responsibility for the outcome, e.g. individual Russian citizens in relation to the social system of soviet communism or individual United States citizens in relation to capitalism in the United States.

An institutional role occupant who fails in his institutional duty by making what is only a tiny causal contribution to some morally untoward outcome, nevertheless, might be held fully institutionally responsible for the outcome and, as a result, fully morally responsible for the outcome; or at least he might only enjoy a minor diminution in moral responsibility, and certainly not a moral diminution commensurate with his very minor share of natural responsibility for the outcome, e.g. a corporate polluter or a person who breaches confidentiality without malevolent intent or a rogue trader who contributes to the collapse of a bank.

At this point we need to introduce the notion of a layered structure of joint action. This is because the analysis of the actions of organized groups and organizations requires the notion of a layered structure of joint actions. Suppose a number of actions are performed by a corporate regulator and his subordinates in order to realize some collective end, e.g. to investigate successfully the corrupt management team of a corporation. This is a joint action. However, it has component joint actions. So there are two levels of joint action.

At level one we have (say) three joint actions each with its own collective end, e.g. a team of auditors checking financial reports, a team of computer forensic investigators examining electronic communications, and a legal team preparing the legal case on the basis of the evidence unearthed.

Each of these three (level one) joint actions is itself describable as an individual action performed (respectively) by the different teams, e.g. the audit, the production of the transcript of communications, the preparation of the brief of evidence.

Each of these three joint actions is itself a component element of a single larger joint action directed to the collective end of successfully investigating the corrupt management of the corporation. This is because each of these joint – now 'individual' – actions is part of a larger plan coordinated by the leadership of the regulator. So these 'individual' actions constitute a level two joint action directed to the collective end of successfully investigating the corrupt management team.

If all, or most, of the individual actions of the members of the corporate regulator (the three teams and their leader) were performed in accordance with collective ends, if the performance of each of the resulting level one joint actions was in accordance with the collective end of successfully investigating the corrupt management team, and if the actions were morally significant then, at least in principle, we could ascribe joint moral responsibility for the outcome to the individual members of the three teams and their leader.

So agents involved in complex, morally significant, cooperative enterprises can, at least in principle, be ascribed collective – i.e. joint – moral responsibility for the outcomes aimed at by those enterprises.

When it comes to corporate corruption, for example, there is a joint responsibility on the part of corporate officers and employees, governments, regulators, auditors, and corruption investigators etc. to eliminate or reduce it. A principal institutional entity in this regard is, as we have argued, the integrity system.

However, in relation to integrity systems, it is necessary to devise institutional mechanisms, if they do not exist, to determine the loci of individual and collective moral responsibility. This process is one of institutionalizing ethical responsibility.

The process can involve an institutional division of labour in relation to a pre-existing diffuse collective moral responsibility, e.g. creating a corporate regulator to combat corporate corruption. Here, the individual members of the corporate regulator come to have a well-defined joint (collective) moral responsibility in relation to combating (say) corporate crime.

Sometimes this process does not involve identifying a pre-existing source of ethical responsibility; rather it involves creating a locus of institutional responsibility to deal with a newly identified ethical problem. An example is the ethical problem of lawyers housed in incorporated, multi-disciplinary practices; such lawyers have potentially conflicting obligations to the courts and to their shareholders. The proposed solution was the creation of the new institutional role of a solicitor-director (see Chapter 6).

In sum, (first point) the notion of collective moral responsibility is to be understood as that of the joint moral responsibility of individual human persons, e.g. the joint responsibility of the members of the board of directors of a corporation, of the members of the enterprise as a whole (officers and employees), of the shareholders, of the members of an external regulatory agency, and so on and so forth.

Moreover, (second point) pre-existing vague and diffuse collective moral responsibilities can be transmogrified – institutionalized – into a system of individual and collective institutional responsibilities that constitutes a set of well-defined, substantive and integrated individual and collective *moral* responsibilities, e.g. of regulators, market actors.

Corporations, Financial Markets and Market Actors

Notwithstanding the general features of integrity systems for institutions adumbrated above, any given integrity system for an institution must be tailored to the needs of that particular institution.[5]

Arguably, market actors, including financial service providers, present a number of relatively distinct problems when it comes to devising integrity systems to ensure ethical practice and the pursuit of ethical ends; or, at any rate, this assumption is a source of the following speculations concerning the integrity system or systems for these groups.

In the first place, and as noted above, market actors do not have an ethical purpose as their proximate end; rather, they have some commercial end, such as profit maximization. The ultimate end is one provided for by the invisible hand. Market actors pursue (individual and collective) self-interest and – by virtue of the workings of the invisible hand – the material well-being of the society is provided for. In this respect, market actors are unlike, say, doctors or hospitals. The latter can reasonably be required to have the promotion of life and health at the forefront of their concerns, i.e. as their proximate as well as ultimate (professional and institutional) ends.

Economic self-interest, especially when linked to social status and power, is a powerful driver, and establishing markets in previously non-market economies, and de-regulating previously heavily regulated market economies, has unleashed a great deal of hitherto dormant human energy. Moreover, the modern corporation as an institution, and the development of global financial markets, has enabled the mobilization of vast capital sums in the service of this human energy. (They have, of course, in turn relied heavily on scientific and technological developments.) One only has to visit Shanghai today and remember what it was like 20 years ago to appreciate the power of market forces (especially government-assisted market forces).

However, from an ethical point of view, the *institutionally structured* self-interested orientation of market actors – including corporations – may well give rise to an immediate problem. How is this institutionally structured impetus and habit of pursuing economic self-interest to be contained within reasonable limits and channelled in appropriate directions? Presumably, this is in part to be achieved by means of some mix of self-regulation and external regulation. However, it is also predicated on the guiding ethico-conceptual frameworks (as opposed to prevailing ideologies) and related self-understandings of these market actors. At any rate, this brings us to a second set of problems.

---

5 An earlier version of the material in this section appeared in Miller, S., 'Institutions, Integrity Systems and Market Actors', in J. O'Brien (ed.), *Private Equity, Corporate Governance and the Dynamics of Capital Market Regulation,* London: Imperial College of London Press, 2007, pp. 297–327.

It is one of the principal tasks of those who design and oversee the market system, including governments and – under the direction of governments – regulators, to ensure that the ultimate purposes of markets (and, therefore, market actors) are in fact achieved, i.e. to contain and channel the pursuit of economic self-interest. Perhaps there is a lack of clarity in the collective minds of governments and regulators in relation to their role in this regard. Politicians these days sometimes talk as if the market were an intrinsic good, i.e. good in itself and independently of its outcomes in terms of human material well-being. But in the view elaborated above, markets need to be conceived in purely instrumentalist terms; they are simply a means to an (ultimate) end (even if this is not the end pursued by the market actors themselves).

Moreover, if one looks, for example, at the objectives of many regulators one typically finds only limited aims, e.g. to reduce crime and protect consumers, and procedural concerns, e.g. to promote competition and efficiency.[6] There is little or no reference to what I have been referring to as the ultimate ends of markets, i.e. the outcome the invisible hand is supposed to bring about. Rather, the image of regulation is one in which regulators are umpires whose sole job is to impartially enforce the rules of the game. But in games, the pleasure of playing aside, there is only one end, namely winning, and this is an end pursued by the players not the umpires. But here the analogy between markets and games breaks down; markets, unlike games, have an end beyond 'winning'; they have ultimate, as opposed to proximate, ends. In the case of markets, 'winning', e.g. making a profit, is only a proximate end and, as such, a means to a further and larger purpose, namely, the material well-being of the society (both national and, in the case of international financial markets, global).

Further, there is the problem mentioned above of the ambiguous role of national governments and regulators when it comes to global markets, including global financial markets. National governments and their regulators are to some extent partisan, and (understandably) seek to look after the economic interests of their own industries and businesses, including their financial service providers. Moreover, in the absence of a uniform set of global regulations and a single global regulator with real authority, regulators operating at a national level can be played off against one another by multi-national corporations.

---

6 The Australian Consumer and Competition Commission, for example, is concerned among other things with the traditional professions but appears to have little or no focus on the distinctive ethical ends of the traditional professions, such as legal practitioners, as compared with other occupational groups. See Alexandra, A., Campbell, T., Cocking, D., Miller, S., and White, K., *Professionalisation, Ethics and Integrity: The Promotion of Professional Ethical Standards and the Protection of Clients and Customers*, Report for the Professional Standards Council, 2006 pp. 1–185. Incidentally, we are not blaming regulators here; they can only carry out the tasks governments give them and resource them to do.

In the case of the global financial sector, regulation and integrity assurance are ultimately in the hands of national governments. However, national governments – and their regulatory authorities – are not simply umpires, they are also players in the financial – and, more generally, corporate – 'game'. For example, the UK government – and its financial regulator (the Financial Services Authority) – cannot be expected to regulate entirely impartially in the interests of ethical ends and principles, given the substantial interest the UK government has in ensuring that the UK corporate and financial sector retains and increases the benefits accruing to it from global financial markets.

A third set of problems confronting the establishment of an integrity system or systems for some market actors, perhaps especially corporations and financial service providers, pertains to the professions. Lawyers and accountants have important roles to play in the integrity systems of corporations, including financial service providers. For, example, auditors conduct audits in order to determine financial propriety and performance, and enable disclosure thereof to regulators and shareholders. However, in many cases auditors and auditing firms appear to have become themselves predominantly market actors, driven principally by the proximate goal of economic self-interest. Arguably, they have (perhaps unconsciously) sought to mask this – and limit their exposure to civil litigation – by taking refuge in compliance with technical procedural requirements, e.g. the accounting rules, in preference to a moral commitment to substantive ethical principles, e.g. a true and fair record.[7] At any rate, the status of auditors as independent professional adjudicators of, for example, financial health, has been significantly compromised. To this extent an important element in the integrity system for corporations has been weakened.[8]

Perhaps there is a fourth problem pertaining to various specific unethical practices, such as insider trading and conflicts of interest; one that derives in part from the de-coupling of ultimate ethical purposes from the self-understanding of market actors, and from the regulation of market actors by governments and their regulatory agencies. The unethical practices in question are not *mala in se*; they are not bad in themselves.

Consider insider trading. Insider trading is not bad in itself as, for example, murder is bad in itself. Rather, insider trading is only morally problematic in a particular institutional context. Now assume that one holds the view, putting it crudely, that markets exist only to further the self-interest of market actors, e.g. to maximize profit or return to shareholders. Why not, then, engage in some insider trading, given that it is in one's self-interest, i.e. it is financially very rewarding

---

7 Clarke, F.G., Dean, G.W., and Oliver, K.C., *Corporate Collapse: Regulatory, Accounting and Ethical Failure*, Cambridge: Cambridge University Press, 1998, p. 319.

8 In addition, it might be that auditors are not well-prepared to detect fraud. See Hodson, N. 'Why Auditors Can't Find Fraud', in J. O'Brien (ed.), *Private Equity, Corporate Governance and the Dynamics of Capital Market Regulation*, London: Imperial College of London Press, 2007.

and it is not easily detected. It might be replied that one should not do so because one is breaking the rules, indeed the law. But unlike murder, insider trading is not morally wrong in itself. Compliance with the law is reinforced by strong moral sentiment, but equally compliance is reduced in the absence of strong moral sentiment. And so, if the practice is not bad in itself, the attitude may take hold; if one can get away with it, why not do it?

Perhaps fair competition is the ethical issue here? But competition in the corporate sector is inevitably unfair; appeals to fairness may (reasonably enough) carry little moral weight. Rather, the substantive moral objection to insider trading is presumably that, in the long run, if enough people practice it, then it undercuts the ultimate, not simply the proximate, ends of the corporate sector.[9] Without compliance with a set of rules or laws that promote competition, the market will not deliver the outcomes promised by the invisible hand. However, this ultimate purpose of markets is not in the forefront of the minds of market actors, preoccupied as they are, and need to be, with the proximate ends of generating profit or maximizing shareholder value.[10] This is perhaps especially the case in the financial services sector, for this sector is arguably at a double remove from the ultimate purposes of the market as a whole; in accordance with the invisible hand it seeks to provide finance to firms that in turn – and again in accordance with the invisible hand – generate the products actually required for the material well-being of the wider society. But if sight is lost of this ultimate purpose – in the self-understanding of market actors and in the policymaking of/regulation by governments and regulators – then perhaps insider trading is bound to be viewed by market actors as much less serious an ethical (as opposed to legal) offence than in reality it is.

A fifth set of issues arise from various perverse incentives that can exist in local and global markets, including financial markets. Competition, including competitive markets, can and does provide discipline to market actors. However, this is not necessarily or always the case. Consider the so-called tragedy of the commons in which everyone pursuing their self-interest destroys the environment. Again consider bribery. It might be the case that for most corporations in some sector bribing officials is necessary in order to be competitive, given that even a small number of other corporations will engage in this practice. Compliance with a legally enforced ethical principle might be in a market actor's self-interest, but only if the enforcement mechanisms are such that everyone (or most) comply. Similarly, there might be competitive pressure to invest in unethical corporations, given the highly lucrative returns, and given that one's competitors are doing so.

9 In fact, some have argued that insider trading should not be a legal offence, since if it was allowed it would not have harmful consequences.

10 On the other hand, we do not accept the proposition that market actors need not have any understanding nor pay any heed to the larger ultimate purposes of markets. The latter attitudes on the part of market actors can lead to an attitude of, for example, breaking the law if one can get away with it.

Again, when liability does not appropriately track ethical responsibility this can lead to perverse incentives. An incentive structure, for example, in which market actors are allowed, indeed encouraged, to take great financial risks with other people's money in order to achieve enormous financial benefits for themselves (and not simply for the investors and shareholders), yet can do so without commensurate legal and financial liability attaching to themselves in the case of things going wrong, is surely tailor-made for corruption. Accordingly, there is a need for institutional re-design of a kind that either decreases the potential financial benefits to such market actors, or increases their liability, or introduces some mixture of both.

More generally, the collective responsibilities of industries to realize their institutional purposes, including the collective responsibilities of financial service providers in capital markets, typically consist of highly dispersed individual responsibilities that attach to individual persons within firms, individual firms within the industry, institutions without the industry, and so on and so forth. The collective responsibility, for example, to lower the cost of capital is not one that can be discharged by any one actor, or even a small group of actors, within a given capital market. Given the diffuse character of such collective responsibilities – and the attendant incentive structure – many industries, financial service providers included, will not discharge these collective responsibilities and, as a consequence, these industries will not adequately realize their institutional purposes. Hence the need (and resultant responsibility) on the part of governments, in particular, to intervene to adjust these incentive structures and, if necessary, to design-in appropriate institutions or sub-elements thereof.

Perverse incentive structures can be addressed by recourse to interventions that reconfigure the incentive structures.[11] Such interventions can take the form of solving jurisdictional problems in global settings, and increasing enforcement options and/or the intensity of enforcement. Thus, Joseph Stiglitz suggests that, 'Any country in which the corporation (or the substantial owners of the corporation) has assets should provide a venue in which suits can be brought or in which enforcement actions to ensure payment of liabilities can be undertaken. The corporation may incorporate where it wants, but this should not make it any less accountable for its actions in other jurisdictions.'[12] In addition, he suggests global widening of the possibility of class action in relation to corporate price-fixing. While obviously of great importance these jurisdictional and enforcement methods are not always sufficient. Other options are themselves market based, e.g. reduce the supply of a product or service by factoring in real costs (and requiring that they be paid), and reduce demand for a product by high sales tax or limiting availability. Some of

11 See Rose-Ackerman, S., *Corruption and Government: Causes, Consequences and Reform*, New York: Cambridge University Press, 1999, for a variety of types of prescription, including adjusting incentive structures, in relation to corruption.

12 Stiglitz, J., *Making Globalization Work: The Next Steps to Global Justice*, London: Penguin, 2006, pp. 206–208. Stiglitz has other suggestions in this regard.

these options involve ambitious innovations to the market system itself, including the global financial system. For example, Stiglitz has proposed a radical extension of the concept of Special Drawing Rights to create a new global reserve currency that would help stabilize financial markets and also make reserves available for wealth creation projects in impoverished countries, increasing literacy, reducing poverty-related diseases, addressing global warming and other 'ultimate' market ends.[13] Still other options are based on the importance of reputation to the self-interest of market actors, e.g. ethics reputational indices might be established to seek to draw attention to their unethical practices or orientations (see Chapter 5).

A sixth and final cluster of problems derives in part from the foregoing ones, and pertains to education, ethos and ideology. If the prevailing ethos or culture of an organization, and perhaps even ideology of central elements of a sector, downplays ethical considerations in favour of self-interest then it should hardly surprise when self-interest overrides compliance with ethical principles, even ones enshrined in the law. This is no doubt especially the case in a context of high temptation and opportunity, on the one hand, and low risk of detection and conviction, on the other, e.g. insider trading in some corporate settings. The point here is not that the majority of individuals themselves engage in corrupt or unethical practices, but rather that in certain cultural or ideological contexts they may well refrain from reporting or otherwise preventing a minority from doing so. Many key elements of integrity systems, such as ethics codes, codes of practice, education programs and the like, do not exist for the most part directly to prevent or deter the few people who are wrongdoers from doing wrong, but rather to ensure that the many are intolerant of the wrongdoing of the few. In this context it is perhaps worth pointing out that most fraudsters are detected and convicted as a consequence of the disclosures of their colleagues.

---

13 Stiglitz, J., *Making Globalization Work: The Next Steps to Global Justice*, London: Penguin, 2006, Chapter 9.

Chapter 3
Codes of Ethics

Ethics and Codes of Ethics

Codes of Ethics are concerned with ethics and, as we have seen, ethics – or morality – is about what actions an individual person or member of an occupation ought to do, and it is about what kind of character an individual person or member of an occupation ought to have.[1] It is also about what features the organizations that employ members of specific occupations ought to have.[2]

Since ethics is not the same thing as etiquette or manners, codes of ethics should not address issues of politeness. Moreover, ethics is not the same thing as aesthetics. Codes of ethics, therefore, should not address issues of style, rhetoric or self-presentation.

Even where occupations deliver moral goods, and consist of the exercise of skills that are virtues because they enable these moral goods to be provided, there would be little point in detailing all these skills, let alone all the accompanying technical knowledge, in the codes of ethics of these occupations. Codes of ethics are not supposed to be exhaustive or comprehensive descriptions of the tasks and knowledge necessary to perform a given occupational role.

Codes of ethics should not attempt to detail specific skills or knowledge that might be necessary to undertake an occupation successfully. For example, public speaking skills are necessary in order to be a successful barrister; but these skills ought not to be detailed in a code of ethics.

Moreover, codes of ethics ought not to address ethical or moral issues that are irrelevant to, or outside the sphere of, the duties, tasks and role of the occupation in question. For example, a practitioner's lawful sexual practices ought not to be an issue addressed in most codes of ethics.

As noted in the introduction to this book, the terms 'ethics' and 'morality' are to be distinguished so that morality refers to minimum standards, whiles ethics refers to a wider field of value that embraces notions of what is good and worth aspiring to – ideals as well as minimum standards.

Accordingly, codes of ethics will refer not only to moral principles, but also to ideals of the good. One important point to consider in this connection concerns punitive sanctions. Presumably, punitive sanctions – sanctions applied in the

---

1 An earlier version of the material in this chapter appeared in Miller, S., *Model Code of Ethics*, Sydney: Professional Standards Council, 2002.

2 For a valuable introduction to codes of ethics see Coady, M., and Bloch, S. (eds), *Codes of Ethics and the Professions*, Melbourne: Melbourne University Press, 1996.

context of an appropriate complaints and discipline system – ought only to be deployed in relation to minimum standards (morality) but not in relation to ideals (ethics). A second important point concerns education. If ideals are to be realized then they need to be inculcated. If this is not to be done primarily by punitive sanctions, it will need to be done (at least in large part) by formal and informal education.

As we saw in the introduction, in thinking and reasoning about moral or ethical questions, and about codes of ethics, we need also to distinguish between actions, habits and attitudes.

If we now turn to ethical actions, as opposed to merely morally acceptable actions, then we can see that they tend to be actions in conformity with ideals or aspirations. For example, giving bread to a hungry person, or not taking advantage of one's competitor when they are in an unfortunate situation owing to bad luck.

Notwithstanding the distinction between minimum standards and ideals, the boundary between these is blurred; there is a considerable grey area. Moreover, again as noted in the introduction, attending only to minimum standards – being a 'rule addict' and eschewing ideals – is problematic: rule addicts lose sight of the values, including ideals, that inform even the rules embodying minimum standards, and this is corrosive of conformity to minimum standards, as well as the realization of ideals.

Codes of ethics typically prescribe and proscribe actions. Indeed, codes of ethics are largely about actions. However, the view that codes of ethics are simply rules that prescribe what actions are to be performed, and what actions are not to be performed, is too narrow. For one thing, codes of ethics typically mention virtues and vices, as well as actions. Virtues and vices are habits or dispositions to act. As such, they are not simply actions; they are elements of a person's character. For another thing, codes of ethics are, or ought to be, concerned with affective attitudes as well as actions. Attitudes are important; attitudes motivate actions.

As we saw in the introduction, habits are dispositions to action that are typically or standardly performed by a person. Habits include virtues, such as courage, honesty and determination, as well as vices, such as cowardice, corruption and dishonesty. Some habits are neither virtues nor vices. As noted above, the key property of virtues and vices is that they are elements of character; they are to do with what a person is, as opposed to what a person might do on some particular occasion. Clearly character, and thus virtues and vices, are of central importance in ethics, and typically they feature in codes of ethics. For example, many codes of ethics advocate the virtue of honesty, trustworthiness, sincerity, and so on.

Affective attitudes, including feelings and emotions, are not actions as such; nor are they habits or merely dispositions to act. A person can obey all the rules, even do so as a matter of habit, and yet have a 'bad attitude'.

Codes of ethics have typically been much more concerned with actions than with attitudes. That said, the so-called caring occupations, such as child-minders, social workers and nurses, typically mention attitudes, such as caring or being sympathetic. So do some other codes, such as journalists' codes. These often note the need for sensitivity in, for example, interviewing someone who has recently suffered trauma. Moreover, even the accountants' codes speak of a duty of care. Doubtless, this duty of care is in large part spelled out in terms of actions. However, it is difficult to conceive of this duty to care as not having at least a partial attitudinal element. A similar point holds for the duty of impartiality.

A further important point that should be made in relation to codes of ethics and attitudes concerns culture or ethos. The culture or ethos of an occupational group or organization is the 'spirit' that pervades it. A group can be said to have a low rather than high morale, or to have a positive culture rather than a culture of complaint, or to have a culture of service rather than one of contempt for the clients. Culture in this sense refers in large part to the attitude of the members of the group to one another and to their clients or customers. It goes without saying that culture in this sense is very often a question of ethical attitude, and therefore ought to fall within the purview of codes of ethics.

The notion of a principle or rule is fundamental to ethics and especially morality, especially in relation to actions. Here we need to distinguish between moral or ethical principles and goals or ends. We also need to distinguish between moral or ethical principles and other sorts of principles.

Goals or ends, including ideals, are states of affair or outcomes that individuals or groups or organizations aim at or seek to realize by means of their actions. Ideals and aspirations are goals or ends that are good, or at least believed to be good. Principles, by contrast, govern actions, not as ends to their means, but as rules or maxims to instances of conformity to them. As such, principles prescribe regularities in action.

The proximate or immediate justification for the existence of many occupations is the existence of a widespread desire, and therefore economic demand, for the product or services that they provide. The justification for ice cream sellers is that people desire to eat ice creams. Presuming such desires not to be harmful – as opposed to harmful desires such as a desire to inject heroin – then the fulfilment of these desires is a good thing, and the product that fulfils them can be referred to as a good, although not necessarily a moral good.

However, the ultimate justification for the existence of human institutions and of associated occupations, such as government, the education system, the health system, the economic system and the criminal justice system, is their provision of some moral or ethical or moral good or goods to the community.[3] The existence of universities is justified by the fact that the academics that they employ discover, teach and disseminate the fundamental human good – knowledge. The existence of governments is justified by the fact that they provide the fundamental social good – leadership of the community – and thereby contribute to prosperity, security, equitable distribution of economic goods, and so on. The existence of an

3 Miller, S., *The Moral Foundations of Social Institutions: A Philosophical Study*, New York: Cambridge University Press, 2009, Chapter 2.

economic system is justified by the fact that it provides for the material well-being of members of the communities that participate in that system.

In short, the point of having any one of these institutions is an ethical or moral one; each provides some fundamental human or social good(s). And the extent to which some specific government or university or economic system fails to provide the moral good that justifies its existence is the extent to which its continued existence needs to be called into question.

In relation to occupations, consider the academics, business people, bureaucrats, doctors, psychiatrists, police officers, journalists, and so on, who abandoned the principles and ideals of their chosen occupations, and put their knowledge and skills in the service of the evil ends of a totalitarian government during the Nazi period.[4]

Closer to home, consider the failure of lawyers, accountants, company directors, economic journalists and politicians to meet the minimum moral standards of their occupations during the 1980s, the period of Bond, Scase and the other 'bold riders' – and the consequent financial ruination of large numbers of ordinary Australians[5] – and more recently during the current financial crisis (see Chapter 2).

Problem solving strategies and policies need to be framed in relation to the fundamental ends or goals of the institution or relevant associated occupations; which is to say they need to be contrived and implemented on the basis of whether or not they will contribute to transforming the institution or relevant associated occupations in ways that will enable it to provide, or better provide, the good(s) – especially moral good(s) – which ultimately justify its existence.

What of principles, as opposed to ends? Examples of moral/ethical principles are: 'Tell the truth', 'Do not break your promises' and 'Do not murder'. Examples of legal rules are: 'Do not steal', 'Do not murder', 'Drive on the right-hand side of the road'. An example of natural scientific principles is 'Speed = distance/ time', and of a social scientific principle is 'Systems of government tend towards oligarchy' (rule by the few). Examples of rules in games include, 'Don't pass the ball forward' (rugby) and 'Don't kick the ball into your own goal' (soccer). An example of a rule of thumb is, 'Look to the right, look to the left and look to the right again before crossing the street'. Principles and rules are concerned with generality, that is, with types of action or event as distinct from one-off actions or events, e.g. 'Do not tell lies' (principle) rather than 'Do not tell John a lie here and now'.

Normative principles are concerned with what is good/bad, what ought and ought not to be, e.g. 'People who are sick ought to go to bed', 'Good administrators only make changes to the procedures if they have a good reason to do so' (stability is a virtue in administration). Notice that ethical or moral principles are one, but

4 Adams, G., and Balfour, D., *Unmasking Administrative Evil*, London: Sage Publications, 1998.

5 Sykes, T., *The Bold Riders*, Sydney: Allen and Unwin, 1994.

only one, species of normative principle. Other kinds of normative principle are prudential and aesthetic normative principles.

Moral and ethical normative principles are concerned with what a person ought to do or ought to be, and with what an organization ought to do or become. For example, 'Individuals ought to tell the truth', and 'Organizations ought to reduce corruption'. Here we can usefully distinguish between rules, conventions and social norms. Codes of ethics are comprised of rules that embody moral norms.[6]

A *rule* is a (typically explicitly formulated) directive issued by some authority or other to undertake a certain course of action in certain recurring situations. So laws are a species of rule enacted by governments. A convention is a regularity in action performed by a set of individual agents and directed to a collective end. Somewhat more precisely, conventions are *joint procedures*, where a procedure is (roughly speaking) a habit, the automatic repetition of an action in a recurring situation. So a joint procedure is a procedure that is jointly followed because it realizes a collective end.

Moreover, on this conception conventions *qua* conventions are normatively neutral, other than in the minimal sense involved in instrumental rationality. Conventions are normatively neutral notwithstanding the fact that agents can be held to have failed to conform to any given convention. In this account, a conventional regularity in action does not constitute a *standard of behaviour* to which agents *ought* to conform. Naturally, an agent, by not conforming, might fail to realize the collective end that he has, the end that is realized by conformity to the convention. However, that would be a mere failure of instrumental rationality.

Therefore, conventional actions are not necessarily the content of directives issued by authorities. Nor are they necessarily explicitly formulated anywhere. Thus, driving on the left-hand side is a convention in Australia, although not in Germany; it is a regularity in action among Australians, which secures the collective end of avoiding car collisions. As it happens, this convention is also a law, although it might not have been.

Social norms are regularities that are also norms; agents believe that they have a duty to conform or that they otherwise *ought* to conform. Such norms include ones respecting and enforcing rights. Here, the 'ought' is not that of mere instrumental rationality; it is not simply a matter of believing that one ought to conform because it serves one's purpose. Some conventions and most rules are also norms in this strong sense. For example, the convention and the law to drive on the left is a norm; and people feel that they ought to conform. This strong (and wide) sense of 'ought' includes, but is not exhausted by, the so-called *moral* ought. Members of some social groups feel strongly about, for example, *aesthetic* requirements; accordingly, the aesthetic 'ought' underpins some of their norms of action. Codes of ethics for occupations comprise, in part, rules that embody social

6 Miller, S., *Social Action: A Teleological Account*, New York: Cambridge University Press, 2001, Chapters 2 and 3.

norms, i.e. accepted moral principles, albeit the moral principles accepted by a particular occupational group for the conduct of their constitutive activities.

Some of moral or ethical principles are forward looking in that they draw attention to future consequences of actions, e.g. 'Do not drink and drive'. Other moral or ethical principles are backward looking in that they draw attention to the motivations or intentions that caused the action or state of affairs, e.g. 'You are morally entitled to the service for which you have paid'.

Some principles are concerned with the nature of actions in themselves (irrespective of motivations or consequences), e.g. the principle not to murder the innocent.

Some principles are not concerned (or not only concerned) with the rightness or wrongness of actions but with the goodness or badness of persons. These moral principles draw attention to a number of elements of moral decision making that are governed by principles, including: character; motivation; intention; action considered on its own; consequences of action.

Affective attitudes are important when it comes to actions. Some actions are regarded as bad/good or moral/immoral partly in virtue of the goodness of badness of the attitudes that motivated them. For example, if a client is disadvantaged by a bureaucrat who acts out of resentment or dislike, this makes the action seem worse than if it were the result of an honest and understandable mistake.

Affective attitudes, including feelings and emotions, are motivations for action and for habits, e.g. 'I killed him (action) out of revenge' (motivation), 'I am honest (habit) because I fear imprisonment' (motivation).

Affective attitudes are themselves sometimes caused by beliefs, including the belief that an action is right or wrong, e.g. the belief that John stole the old blind lady's purse or that John is a coward causes the attitude of dislike/contempt for John. Further, attitudes are sometimes caused by habits or dispositions, e.g. a dishonest disposition causes disgust with oneself.

Like actions, habits and attitudes can be changed, albeit over time; for instance, a sloppy and uncaring worker in an occupation or organization with a dysfunctional culture might become a careful and concerned worker in a different working environment.

In so far as codes of ethics are devices that can be used to reinforce desirable behaviour and change undesirable behaviour – albeit devices that need to be used in conjunction with complaints and discipline systems, appropriate structures of reward, effective processes of conflict resolution, ethics education programmes, and so on – then they need to attend not simply to the behaviour (action) itself, but also to the character (habits) and affective attitudes that condition and motivate that behaviour.

Codes of ethics typically prescribe and proscribe actions, habits and attitudes. So far so good. However, at least two questions arise. The first question concerns the reason or reasons for prescribing some action or other. Sometimes codes do provide reasons for their prescriptions. But in general the code is too brief to elaborate the various reasons. Nevertheless, reasons ought to be given. Hence the need for a bare code of ethics to be supplemented by explanatory material.

The second question concerns what to do when prescriptions and principles, which are desirable in themselves, nevertheless come into conflict in some particular situation. As noted in the introduction, there is a need for a rationally motivated balance to be struck. Accordingly, there is a need for a process of rational reflection.

Some codes of ethics are supplemented by a model of practical moral reasoning, e.g. the code of professional conduct of the Institute of Chartered Accountants of Australia, and of the Certified Practising Accountants. There are a number of such models of reasoning available in the applied philosophical literature, some more adequate than others. It is desirable that codes of ethics be supplemented by a sound model of practical moral reasoning in order to facilitate the application of the codes.

As we noted in the introduction, notwithstanding the fact that law and morality are not necessarily the same thing, it is nevertheless true – at least in the case of the criminal law – that law and morality often coincide. The moral rights enshrined in the criminal law are those ones regarded as fundamental by the wider society; they constitute the basic moral norms of the society.

In light of the above, a question arises as to whether all or most codes of ethics ought to say something about obedience to the law. Some, such as many solicitors and police codes of ethics, already do. Other occupations not closely involved with upholding the law, such as the code of the National Institute of Forensic Engineers, also state that the law should be upheld.

Codes of ethics are a good place for occupations to signal their commitment to the basic laws, and thus basic moral standards, of the community to which they belong, and to which they contribute. Moreover, in this connection it is important for occupations to express their commitment to the cornerstone principle of a free society, namely the principle of individual autonomy. Individual autonomy comprises various freedoms, including freedom of speech and thought, freedom of movement, and freedom to work and to do so for reasonable remuneration.

As we noted in Chapter 1, there is an important distinction to be made between professions and other professional groups. If indeed professions are a distinctive form of occupation with the defining features described in Chapter 1, then this will need to be reflected in their codes of ethics. Since the telos or end of the work of the professions is a moral good, then this should to be stressed in their codes of ethics, as should the distinctive rights of professional practitioners, e.g. professional autonomy. Again, given the role of the professional associations, the code of ethics of members of the professions will need to have sanctions built into them.

History of Codes of Ethics

Codes of ethics belong to that family of texts, including written oaths, rule-books, codes of practice and the like, wherein the members of some group put forth a set of requirements, and perhaps aspirations, and commit themselves to act in accordance with these requirements.

So a code of ethics has two aspects: (1) the *content*, comprising the requirements, rules, principles, ideals, and so forth; (2) the *commitment* of the members of the occupation or organization to conform to, and otherwise uphold, those rules and ideals.

What we have called the content of the code ought to reflect the proper ends or goals of the occupation, as well as the reasonable constraints on the activities undertaken in pursuit of those ends. The commitment to that content on the part of the members of the occupation consists of an oath, or promise, or other kind of undertaking that each member has given to adhere to the code.

Historically, the term 'code' has applied to such diverse texts as the Code of Hammurabi (18th century BC), the Priestly Code (of the Old Testament), the Hippocratic Oath (fifth century BC – for medical practitioners), monastic codes of the middle ages, e.g. Benedict's Rule, the rule of the Knights Hospitallers of St John of Jerusalem (during the Crusades) and the Code Napoleon (1804–10).

So priest, monks and knights have provided themselves with codes for centuries. And these codes typically consisted of a commitment to some or other variety of ethical content; so they can be more or less regarded as codes of ethics.

As far as the professions, in particular, are concerned, lawyers and doctors, of a kind, existed in ancient Greece and Rome.[7] Medicine became a full-blown profession before law. Medicine emerged as a profession in the early Christian era.

During the dark ages, medical knowledge – and indeed legal and other knowledge – was preserved in the monastic orders. Following the establishment of universities in the medieval period, knowledge and learning, including that pertaining to the professions, gradually broke free from the Church and underwent a process of secularization. In the early 16th century, professional and other associations – essentially elite guilds – were formed and confirmed by the monarchs of the day, practitioners were issued licences, entry restrictions were imposed, high fee structures introduced, judges, doctors and others professionals were drawn from their ranks, and so on. The basis for the modern professions was laid.

In 1794, Thomas Percival proposed a code of ethics for physicians and surgeons in England. In 1808 the Boston Medical Society put forward a code of ethics. By the early part of the 20th century codes of ethics were in place in most of the traditional professions in the US, and in due course the possession of a code of ethics became a defining feature of being a profession.

---

7 Siggins, I., 'Professional Codes: Some Historical Antecedents', in M. Coady, and S. Bloch (eds), *Codes of Ethics and the Professions*, Melbourne: Melbourne University Press, 1996.

In the latter part of the 20th century, codes of ethics for the professions underwent significant changes, as the professions sought to accommodate legal, social and economic changes. In part, these changes reflected the desire of the traditional professions to hold onto their power and status as their members were increasingly housed in large organizations, and subjected to competitive market pressures. Moreover, other occupations, such as journalism, nursing and, recently, policing, aspired to professional status. Accordingly, these emerging 'professions' developed codes of ethics.

A final important development has been the proliferation of codes of ethics among members of occupations who do not necessarily seek to present themselves as among the professions, e.g. real estate valuers, and in organizations who do not even constitute occupations. The latter organizations include both public sector and private sector organizations.

Historically, codes of ethics were an important defining feature of the traditional professions. In Chapter 1, we argued that there was an important distinction to be made between professions and other occupations. This claim is consistent with some occupations emerging as professions; such occupations have come to possess the defining properties of professions. However, the possession of a code of ethics can no longer be regarded as a defining property of the professions. Perhaps this was historically the case; but it is no longer so. Moreover, it is surely desirable for many occupations that are not professions, to nevertheless have a code of ethics. Indeed, it is desirable for many organizations to have a code of ethics.

In short, while historically codes of ethics for occupations may have been the preserve of the professions, this is no longer the case; nor should it be. Codes of ethics are good for the professions; but equally, codes of ethics are good for other occupations.

The Functions of Codes of Ethics: Ethics Education and Ethics Regulation

By presenting in an explicit form the basic ends of an occupation, the rights and duties of the members of the occupation, the constraints on their activity, the rights of clients, and so on, codes of ethics perform an educative function.[8] Knowledge of the code of ethics is knowledge of the ethical ideals and principles pertaining to that occupation, and members of the occupation can and ought to possess that knowledge. This knowledge is principally *practical*, as opposed to theoretical, knowledge. It is knowledge about how to do something, as opposed to knowledge concerning what is the case.

The knowledge expressed in a code is expressed in a condensed form. Accordingly, as already mentioned, there is a need for additional explanatory

---

8 For a useful discussion on functions of codes of ethics, see Lichtenberg, J. 'What are Codes of Ethics for?' in M. Coady, and S. Bloch (eds), *Codes of Ethics and the Professions*, Melbourne: Melbourne University Press, 1996.

material, e.g. regarding the nature and function of the specific occupation in question, and additional tools for applying this knowledge, e.g. a model of practical ethical reasoning. Moreover, this knowledge needs to be suitably contextualized in relation to specific concrete ethical problems that might be confronted by members of that occupational group. So there is also a need for supplementary case studies and the like.

Moreover, since this practical knowledge of ethical principles and ideals, and practical knowledge of their application, is not a static thing – ethical problems and the solutions to them undergo change – there is a need for ongoing revision of the code of ethics, ongoing education in relation to changes to the code of ethics, and especially ongoing education in relation to the application of the principles and ideals expressed in the code of ethics. The code of ethics, and associated ethical education, ought to be an important element in initial formal and informal education programmes, an also in continuing education programmes.

It is important to note that ethical codes not only have content – they are not simply documents that can be the objects of (practical) knowledge – they also involve, or ought to involve, commitment on the part of the members of the occupation or organization in question.

The commitment in question is both personal and collective commitment. Each individual practitioner commits him or herself to the content of the code, or should do so. But each does so on condition the others do so; the individual commitments are interdependent, and therefore collective. Such interdependence of commitment to a common set of ideals and principles is in part constitutive of a self-conscious community of practitioners, and is a necessary condition for that community having an ethical culture. Accordingly, codes of ethics have a function of socio-ethical or cultural integration, as well as of education in the narrow individualistic sense.

In order that that this commitment exists in some tangible form, there is a need at the very least for the individual members of the occupation or organization to participate in the establishment, and ongoing revision, of their code of ethics. Without such participation the code will not be a 'live' document, and it will not be 'owned' by the members of the occupational group or organization.

The process by which a code of ethics is drafted, or redrafted, ought to involve not only consultation regarding the basic principles and ideals, but also research into ethical problems confronted by members, and some attempt to have members ratify or otherwise indicate their acceptance of the code once it is finalized.

Codes of ethics prescribe and proscribe specific actions, and many of them attach sanctions to non-compliance.

Codes of ethics therefore have a regulatory function, in addition to their educative and cultural integration functions. Often, the main regulatory role of a code of ethics is actually played by an associated code of practice. The code of ethics is a basic presentation of principles and ideals; the code of practice is a detailed description of the actions that are to be performed and not performed, and of the sanctions that attach to non-performance.

Be that as it may, here we want to elaborate on the notion of regulation and its relation to ethical behaviour and to ethics education (formal and informal).

Regulation, like ethical education, ought to proceed in such a way as to secure compliance with appropriate moral principles, especially compliance with minimum standards, e.g. avoidance of criminal activity such as fraud, theft, eschewing of unfair practices, and so on.

Moreover, regulation of occupations involved in the market economy ought to promote an efficient, competitive market; and education likewise ought to promote this.

However, regulation of itself, unlike education, is less able to promote pursuit of ideals, as opposed to conformity to minimum standards. This is not to say that the regulative and the educative roles of codes of ethics (or of codes of ethics and codes of practice) are somehow independent of one another, or that they ought to be. Far from it. They ought to be interdependent and mutually reinforcing.

In contriving regulations, account ought to be taken not simply of the self-interested motivations of the relevant actors, but also of their ethical motivations, including not only their sense of fairness and susceptibility to feelings of shame, but also their desire for the respect that goes with achievement of high ideals. This is a general truth that goes as much for codes of ethics and codes of practice, as it does for laws and regulations.

It is worth bearing in mind here that regulations, and the law more generally, are conformed with not only because they have sanctions attached, but also because they are perceived to be fair, and also rational in terms of the ends of the activity regulated. Compliance with unfair or irrational regulations can be very hard to achieve, even if heavy penalties attach to non-compliance. Indeed, it may be that the best regulatory strategies are those in which the fairness and reasonableness of a regulation and the sanctions attaching to it mutually reinforce one another.[9] (See Chapter 2, especially the section on holistic integrity systems.)

Contriving and framing regulations gives rise to a wide array of quite specific ethical problems concerning the fairness of particular practices or reward systems, the ethical unacceptability of some conflicts of interest, and so on. Many of these are complex intellectual problems, and solving them involves not simply the identification of (often competing) ethical considerations, but also the elaboration of new principles that give due weight to these ethical considerations. There is a need for systematic ethical reflection.

Regulations may be too few and too simple, or conversely, too many and too complex. If the former, they might fail to regulate ethically undesirable practices: if the latter, practitioners might be unduly hamstrung, and have to face the consequent moral dilemma of either ignoring regulations, or failing to operate an efficient profitable business. Indeed, if regulations are incomprehensible, then practitioners

9 See Ayres, I., and Braithwaite, J., *Responsive Regulation*, Oxford: Oxford University Press, 1992.

may not be able to discharge their moral obligations to obey the regulations even if they want to.

The general point to be made here if reform in regulations is to be effective is that there needs to be a well-educated and ethically informed community of reflective practitioners – regulation and education, including ethical education, need to go hand in hand. Codes are a useful tool in this regard; for they are, or ought to be, documents that embody both a regulative and an educative function in relation to the basic principles and ideals of an occupation.

Codes of Ethics and the Occupational Context

Codes of ethics should not exist in isolation. If they do, they are unlikely to fulfil their educative, regulatory and integrative functions. As we have already seen, a minimal code of ethics needs to be supplemented by explanatory material, by a model of practical ethical reasoning, by concrete examples of ethical problems and solutions, and possibly by a code of practice.

More generally, codes of ethics, if they are to succeed, need to exist in an environment in which ethics education is taken seriously and undertaken on an ongoing basis.

Further, codes of ethics – and their associated codes of practice – need to exist in an occupational environment in which the systems of reward and of punishment are perceived to be fair and reasonable. Moreover, codes of ethics need to exist in an occupational environment in which they are 'owned' by the members of the occupation in question.

The desire amongst members of an occupation to do what is right can be reinforced by ensuring a just system of rewards and penalties within the occupation or organization. Unfair workloads or financial rewards, unjust systems of promotion, unreasonably harsh disciplinary procedures for minor errors, and so on, are all deeply corrosive of the desire to do one's job well and to resist inducements to do what is illegal or otherwise immoral.

Further, complaints and disciplinary processes need to be transparent, independent and fair. Moreover, they need to be reasonably efficient and effective. If not, they will cease to adequately serve their function, they will be regarded with ambivalence and they will ultimately fall into disrepute.

Fair and effective complaints and disciplinary processes are important, if minimum moral standards are to be maintained. Those who are incompetent, or seek to engage in behaviour in contravention of codes of practice, or behaviour that is corrupt or even unlawful, need to be made accountable and held responsible. However, the logical endpoint of increasing accountability is a huge corpus of regulations, and ongoing and expensive investigative and disciplinary activity.

Moreover, excessive reliance on accountability mechanisms bypasses the issue of moral responsibility, which lies at the heart of corruption and unlawful conduct. In the final analysis, the only force strong enough to resist unacceptable behaviour is the moral sense – the desire to do what is right and avoid doing what is wrong. If most practitioners in a given occupation do not for the most part have a desire to avoid doing what contravenes relevant regulations or laws, or is otherwise immoral, no accountability system – no matter how extensive and elaborate – can possibly suffice to control unacceptable conduct.

The desire to do what is right does not exist independently of the habit of reflection and judgement on particular pressing ethical issues. Accordingly, the desire to do what is right can be reinforced by ensuring that ethical issues are matters of ongoing discussion and reflection in initial training programmes, further education programmes, and in relation to ethical codes.

Further, the desire to do what is right must be reinforced by utilizing the intrinsically collective nature of an occupational group, or of an organization, and in particular by stressing that the members of an occupation are collectively responsible for maintaining the minimum standards. (See the section 'Collective Moral Responsibility and Integrity Systems' in Chapter 2.) It is a mistake to rely on the moral courage of isolated individuals conceived of as being responsible only for their own actions.

In general, if an individual did all that he or she could in the circumstances to avoid performing a wrongful individual action, or contributing to a wrongful joint action, then that individual should not be held responsible or penalized for such actions. However, that is not the end of the matter.

Individual members of an organization or occupation also have ethical responsibilities in relation to the behaviour of individuals other than themselves. Consider a practitioner who becomes aware that one of his or her peers is engaged in unlawful or corrupt or incompetent conduct. Clearly, there is an obligation to do something about this, for example to report the conduct. This individual obligation exists by virtue of a collective responsibility that members of an occupation or organization have to ensure that minimum standards are complied with by all members of the occupation or organization.

Indeed, collective responsibility also entails such actions as reporting infringements of minimum standards, and support for, rather than opposition to, those who report such infringements in good faith.

The collective effort to ensure that there are minimal standards of an occupation – minimum standards enshrined in the code of ethics – will contribute to the internalization by practitioners of those standards. More important, such a collective effort will ensure that practitioners identify with those standards so that self-respect, as well as the respect of others, depends on the maintenance of those standards and on intolerance of those who cannot or will not meet them.

The notion of a 'self-regulating occupation' has a good deal of currency. One meaning for this term is that the members of an occupation establish and run their own accountability systems, including complaints and discipline systems (see Chapter 1, final section). A second meaning is that members of an occupation see to it that infringements of minimum standards are not tolerated; this is not so much a matter of formal processes as of ethical culture and a strong sense of collective responsibility. Whether or not a given occupational group ought to be self-regulating in the first sense, it certainly ought to be self-regulating in the second sense. If it is not self-regulating in this second sense, then it is not likely to be an ethical community of practitioners.[10]

Generic Principles of a Code of Ethics

In earlier sections we have detailed what might be termed the generic functions of codes of ethics, e.g. educative and regulative. We have also detailed the various associated institutional devices and educational tools that need to accompany codes of ethics, if such codes are to be effective. These included additional explanatory material, case studies, models of practical ethical reasoning, ethics components in continuing professional development programmes, codes of practice, and just and reasonable complaints and discipline systems. And we have indicated the kinds of participatory processes that need to be gone through in the drafting and redrafting of codes of ethics. Further, we have described, in suitably general terms, the features of the occupational and organizational context in which codes of ethics would have maximal effect.

It remains to consider the generic content of codes of ethics. Given the diversity of occupations – and we have insisted on a distinction between the professions and other occupations – many of the principles and ideals differ, and ought to differ, from one occupation to another.[11]

Nevertheless, in the context of the conclusions reached above, and in the light of our review of a large number of codes of ethics, a number of important points in relation to the generic content of codes of ethics suggest themselves. Codes of ethics should ideally:

1. Describe not only minimum standards, but also occupational ideals; in so doing they should include not only action guiding principles, but also virtues and desirable attitudes.
2. Contain a statement to the effect that minimum standards ought not to be compromised, even in the face of internal pressure from the occupation or organization to which one belongs or external pressure from outside organizations and groups.

10 Self-regulation as a mark of the professions is controversial. See, for example, Bayles, M.D., 'Professional Power and Self-Regulation', *Business and Professional Ethics Journal*, vol. 5, no. 2, 1986, p. 27; Camenisch, P., 'Business Ethics: On Getting to the Heart of the Matter', *Business and Professional Ethics Journal*, vol. 1, no. 1, 1981, p. 61.

11 In this connection, the Center for the Study of Ethics in the Professions at the Illinois Institute of Technology has made an important contribution in compiling a library of codes (see www.iit.edu/departments/csep/PublicWWW/codes). The library contains 500 codes of ethics.

3. Contain a statement to the effect that members of the occupation or organization ought to obey the just and reasonable laws of the community.
4. Contain a statement expressing a commitment to the principle of individual autonomy (comprising freedom of action, speech, to work, etc.) – the cornerstone of a free society.
5. Contain a statement expressing commitment to non-discrimination on the basis of gender, race, etc.
6. Contain a statement to the effect that members of the occupation or organization ought to obey the just and reasonable regulations governing the activity of the members of the occupation or organization in question.
7. Contain an integrity statement to the effect that members of the occupation or organization ought to avoid telling lies (tell the truth) and do what they say they will do (keep their promises).
8. Set out the fundamental goals or ends of an occupation, as well as the constraints on the pursuit of those ends, e.g. health, law and order, education, provision of housing.
9. Prioritize some of the principles, rights and ideals listed in the code.
10. Set out the principal rights of members of the occupation in relation to salient groups such as employers, peers and clients, e.g. sphere of autonomy in relation to their employers.
11. Contain a statement or statements committing members to respect the relevant rights of consumers and clients, e.g. informed consent in relation to the work to be undertaken and the fees and payments to be charged, and privacy and confidentiality.
12. Contain a statement to the effect that complaints and disciplinary processes ought to conform to principles of independence, reasonableness and fairness.
13. Contain a statement to the effect that members ought only undertake work that they are competent to perform.
14. Contain a statement to the effect that members ought to undertake their work conscientiously, and with efficiency and effectiveness.
15. Contain a statement regarding adequate initial and ongoing education.
16. Contain a statement committing members to compete fairly in the market.
17. Contain a statement expressing the principle that one should build one's professional or occupational reputation on the basis of merit.
18. Address the issue of occupational or organizational culture, e.g. secrecy and closing ranks in relation to wrongdoing or incompetence on the part of peers.
19. Address problematic ethical issues that their members confront, e.g. the appropriate role of the market in relation to the provision of medical services, and conflicts of interest that arise from various sources including role confusion.
20. Contain a statement in relation to the collective responsibility of members to report on any failure of their peers to meet minimum standards.

21. Contain a statement in relation to the need for loyalty and cooperation among members of an occupation in the service of the goals and ideals of the occupation.
22. The ethical issues raised by members of an occupation working in a multi-disciplinary workplace, or working in an organization that might have requirements that are in potential conflict with the requirements of their occupation, need to be addressed in their occupational code of ethics, and/or the codes of ethics of the organizations in question.

Developing a Code of Ethics

The process for developing a code of ethics for an occupation might take the following form.

1. Establishment of Ethics Committee Phase

Establish an Ethics Committee to take responsibility for drafting the code. The committee should involve at least two members from outside the occupation, including a philosopher with expertise in occupational ethics, and at least one person 'representing' the occupation's client or consumer group. Membership of the Ethics Committee should be for a specified term. A degree of continuity of membership is desirable. So provision should be made for only half of the terms of members to expire at the same time.

2. Examination of Issues Phase

The Ethics Committee should:

- Identify the purposes to be served by a code of ethics, e.g. education, regulation.
- Identify the format of the code of ethics, e.g. explanatory material, accompanying code of practice, model of practical reasoning.
- Examine the main goals, activities and context (including organizational context) of the occupation.
- Outline the role of members of the occupational group.
- Detail the main ethical requirements of members of the occupational group.
- Identify the main ethical problems likely to be confronted.
- Prepare a document setting forth the results of the above discussions. This is not a draft code of ethics, but rather a discussion of issues, ethical problems, and ideally a set of case studies and questions.

3. Research Phase

The document prepared by the Ethics Committee should be used in the research involving the members of the occupation and members of salient other groups, e.g. clients. This research would (ideally) involve:

- Survey instruments
- Case studies (pre-existing ones and development of new ones)
- Focus Groups
- Interviews with key informants from outside occupation

4. Drafting of Code of Ethics Phase

In light of the research findings, a draft code of ethics and accompanying material should be prepared by the Ethics Committee.

5. Consultation Phase

All registered members to be sent the draft code of ethics together with a questionnaire to gauge their response in general and to specifics.

6. Ratification of Code of Ethics Phase

The code should be circulated for the purposes of final comment and ratification by members of the occupation or by the relevant representative occupational bodies.

7. Review of Code of Ethics Phase

There should be a formal review of the code of ethics at set intervals by the Ethics Committee. The review should at least involve a Consultation phase in addition to a redrafting by the Committee.

Codes of Ethics as Window-dressing

Unfortunately, there are often fundamental divergences between the reality of everyday practice and the behaviour being recommended in ethical codes; the codes are 'Pollyana-ish'.

Consider the following code of ethics developed by Motorola.

> Key beliefs define who we are – as individuals and as a company. Our key beliefs have defined us for many years to each other, to our customers, our shareholders, our suppliers, our competitors, and our communities.

> Uncompromising integrity means staying true to what we believe. We adhere to honesty, fairness and 'doing the right thing' without compromise, even when circumstances make it difficult.
>
> Constant respect for people means we treat others with dignity, as we would like to be treated ourselves. Constant respect applies to every individual we interact with around the world.
>
> Each of us is expected to demonstrate these key beliefs in our work as Motorolans.[12]

In the case of Motorola, the divergence is between the ethical conduct that managers and employees are supposed to aspire to, and the necessity for the organization to be profitable and competitive in the market place. Such divergences can engender a sense of scepticism in many recipients towards such instruments. The solution appears to be, first, that codes of ethics cease to be mere window-dressing by facing up to real and difficult moral problems, and offering guidance in relation to them; and, second, that where appropriate, employees and others begin seriously to rethink their day-to-day practices in the light of moral principles and ethical concerns.

The second observation is that such codes of ethics necessarily reflect values that are generally accepted in the community. At a very basic level, the terms that they use – such as 'trust', 'ethical', and 'honesty' – have meanings that individuals bring to the context in which they are operating. To a large extent, statements of values are reflective of the underlying moral values of the community from which the employees are drawn, and serve to remind employees that they are also operative in the work context. However, the point about an effective code of ethics – as opposed to a piece of window-dressing – is that it is the result of a process of collective reflection and discussion in which basic community values and moral principles are applied to, and refined in, specific work contexts; the result should be a set of meaningful ethical prescriptions in relation to behaviour and attitudes in the workplace.

Effective codes of ethics facilitate the engagement between pre-existing moral values on the one hand, and the reality of day-to-day practice on the other. That said, even effective statements of values and codes of conduct alone are obviously not sufficient to create an ethical organizational climate. Let us now turn to another key element of effective integrity systems, namely, complaints and discipline systems.

---

12 Motorola website (http://www.motorola.com/code/code.html). Accessed 3 January 2003.

Chapter 4
Complaints and Discipline Systems

The Place of a Complaints and Discipline System

In the previous chapter we looked at the codification of occupational ethical standards in codes of ethics and practice. We pointed out that such codes ideally serve a number of functions, identified as educative, integrative and regulatory. The extent to which any actual code serves these functions is partly a matter of its content and mode of development. But it also depends on the way in which it integrates with other elements of an overall occupational integrity system. Of particular importance here is the existence of a well-designed and functioning complaints and discipline system. There is often a good deal of scepticism, if not downright cynicism, about codes of ethics, which are seen as 'window dressing', among both the general public and members of the occupation itself. While there may be a number of reasons for this, arguably one important reason is the lack of effective responses to breaches of the standards laid down in codes.

This chapter focuses on systems for identifying and responding to such breaches, so-called complaints and discipline systems. In the first part of this chapter we examine these systems; in the second we look more closely at the obstacles that may stand in the way of members of occupations disclosing information that they have about serious wrongdoing.

Like a code of ethics, a complaints and discipline system serves a number of different functions. We outline these in the following section of the chapter then look at the general characteristics such a system will need to have to serve these functions, and provide the outlines of a model complaints and discipline system.

As its name implies there are two components to a complaints and discipline system: first gathering and classifying complaints (the complaint element), then assessing and responding to those complaints that are prima facie grounds for sanctioning a member of the occupation (the discipline element). An effective method for gathering complaints is a necessary condition for a fair discipline system; at the same time, complaints are more likely to be forthcoming if it is perceived that they will be taken seriously and responded to appropriately. Moreover, as we discuss below, the complaint element can serve a number of valuable functions in its own right, apart from providing the material on which the discipline element acts.

Functions

Like all the other elements of an occupational integrity system, the ultimate function of a complaints and discipline system is to assist the members of an occupation achieve its ultimate purpose or goal. While this claim is a truism, it is worth keeping in mind when considering the design and application of specific systems.

The most important immediate function of a complaints and discipline system is to resolve grievances against members of an occupation. These grievances may be held by clients, consumers or by third parties affected by the behaviour of members, or by other occupational members. Some grievances, especially those of clients and third parties, rest on misunderstandings of the responsibilities of the practitioner, the rights of the client and so on; others may be resolved through discussion and negotiation or mediation. In the first instance, then, a complaints and discipline system may resolve grievances through providing information, or directing parties to a dispute towards the resources they need to settle it between themselves.

Where grievances cannot be resolved in these ways, they may need to be dealt with more formally. This may be through the discipline process of the complaints and discipline system, or it may be through a court or some other such forum.

The second function of a complaints and discipline system is the detection of breaches of occupational standards. Here, a distinction can be drawn between unsatisfactory conduct, on the one hand, and ethical misconduct, including corruption and criminality, on the other. Unsatisfactory conduct is conduct that falls short of the standard of competence and diligence that can reasonably be expected of a competent practitioner; for example, as a consequence of carelessness or haste. Misconduct describes more serious breaches of occupational standards. It might involve deliberate wrongdoing, as when a practitioner holds themselves out as possessing qualifications or competencies they do not have, or gives a client false information in order to win a commission or a promotion. It might also involve negligent or reckless breaches of occupational standards that the member should have known were likely to create substantial risks of harm or cost to others. Moreover, a pattern of behaviour might constitute misconduct even though any single element in that pattern by itself would not.

Further functions of the complaints and discipline system are involved in the responses made to breaches of occupational standards. The third function of such a system is to reveal areas in which a member of an occupation who has breached occupational standards needs further development, through training, supervision and the like.

Fourthly, in the case of serious breaches, the system may function to identify matters for criminal investigation by the police, sanction the member for disciplinary breaches, and/or direct them to provide restitution to those harmed by their actions.

Fifthly, the way in which the system processes complaints and responds to demonstrated breaches has an important role in setting and reinforcing professional ethical norms, by demonstrating the kinds of behaviours the profession sees as unacceptable and apt for sanctioning, and how seriously different sorts of breaches are regarded. The treatment of complainants by the complaints and discipline procedure itself sends important messages about the appropriate attitude to take to clients, and to client/member relationships. Moreover, as noted in the previous chapter, codes of ethics and the like tend to be couched in general terms. Members may be enjoined 'to be of good character'. Would being found guilty of engaging in illegal sexual practices show that a teacher was not of good character, for example? The determinations of the panels empowered to adjudicate in complaints, then, in effect specify how the general statements of codes of ethics are to be interpreted in practice.

Finally, a complaints and discipline system has an important function in gathering information for use by individual members of an occupation, occupational settings (such as businesses or public sector agencies) and the occupation as a whole. Data should be collected about the context, nature (e.g. conflict of interest, discourtesy etc.) and frequency of complaints. Aggregated data of sources, kinds and frequency of complaints made, and upheld, can be used to identify ways in which sources of conflict can be removed or reduced (through, for example the development of a pro forma contract), or where professional education is needed, or a public communication strategy needs to be developed or refined (for example, in cases where many complaints are shown to be based on a misunderstanding of the role of the professional), or in which the code of ethics should be reconsidered. Against the background of such data for the occupation as a whole (or relevant sub-groups thereof), information about individuals can be used to identify those who are 'at risk' (who have, say, an unusual number of low-level complaints made against them) and action, such as professional development and/or monitoring, to be taken. Likewise, comparisons of similar occupational settings may reveal anomalous patterns of complaints (i.e. noticeably high or low compared with the norm) indicating the need for further investigation and, perhaps, action. The intelligence gathered through a complaints and discipline system is also an important source for information for an occupation's Ethics Audit (discussed in the next chapter, in the section 'Ethics Audit and Reputation Index'.)

Ideally, a complaints and discipline system will embody all these functions. However, there are a number of difficulties standing in the way of constructing a system that actually does this. Some of these difficulties are generic. For example, there is a tension, at least, between the 'grievance resolution' and 'sanctioning and restitution' functions, where fear of becoming liable for serious sanctioning will act as a disincentive for a practitioner to admit to mistakes, which, in turn, is likely to further fuel a client's sense of grievance.

Some of the difficulties facing an occupational group in constructing a satisfactory complaints and discipline system, on the other hand, will be specific to the group. For example, as discussed in Chapter 1, certain sorts of misconduct may be unlikely to evince complaints from clients. Consider the case of an auditor who is colluding with a large corporate client to sign off on misleading financial statements. (See the discussion of the relationship between Enron and its auditors in Chapter 2.) Or think of a counsellor who is having an affair with one of her clients. Although the counsellor is thereby committing a very serious breach of professional ethics, the client may have no desire to make a complaint, or to cooperate if one is nevertheless made.

Moreover, what might be broadly thought of as an occupational 'culture' might militate against detection of wrongdoing, with colleagues unwilling to lodge complaints against each other, even in cases of egregious wrongdoing, or to treat complaints seriously if they have adjudicative responsibilities. (We discuss some of the issues here further below.)

General Characteristics

From the characterization of the functions of a complaints and discipline system outlined above, we can derive a number of general characteristics that such a system should possess. The overarching requirements are that the system is constructed in such a way as to achieve both procedural and substantive justice. That is, it should have fair, transparent and effective procedures in place that are likely to reveal the truth concerning occupational (mis)conduct, and deliver responses appropriate to that conduct.

Procedural justice, in this context, encompasses more than just the regulations governing the workings of disciplinary tribunals. It also includes the broader 'user-friendliness' of the whole system, such as ease of access, speediness of dealing with complaints, support for participants, and so on, in so far as these affect the substantive justice of the way in which the system deals with wrongdoing. Most occupational associations have, at best, limited investigative powers and lack coercive powers, and depend on volunteers to sit on tribunals. Their complaints and discipline systems, then, are only likely to function effectively if their members, and those affected by members' actions, are willing to participate.

If (potential) complainants perceive that the complaint process is difficult or futile, or that they are likely to be met with hostility, they are obviously less likely to make or proceed with a complaint. That impinges on all the functions of the complaints and discipline system (for example, it distorts information about occupational malfeasance, subverts proper norms regarding practitioner/client relationships, magnifies rather than resolves grievances, and so on). Similarly, if members of occupations perceive that the system is unreasonably harsh (or unreasonably lenient) or selectively applied, they may be less inclined to participate in or support it.

It is, moreover, important to be aware of the ways in which sanctioning can have negative effects that are much more weighty than the formal sanctions themselves. A survey of nurses in New York State who had been disciplined for professional misconduct[1] showed that, overwhelmingly, not only had their careers been adversely affected as a consequence, but so had their health, self-esteem, personal relationships and financial status. Ninety-seven percent reported feelings of shame, the same percentage reported that their health had suffered. Although only 17 percent had lost their licence to practice, almost half no longer worked as nurses. It seems that many of the surveyed nurses who admitted to wrongdoing had done little to prepare for disciplinary proceedings, believing that they should accept 'what they had coming to them'. But they had little understanding of the workings of the system to which they were exposed, or of the possible consequences of a negative finding. In some cases, at least, it appears that they were disproportionately blamed for an outcome for which they were only marginally responsible.[2]

Studies of this kind indicate the need to provide support for subjects of complaints to help them understand the workings of the complaints and discipline system, and the possible implications of the different courses of action available to them. They also illustrate the disadvantages of an adversarial system (as the New York system was), in which one party aims to demonstrate wrongdoing on the part of another, and to exact as severe a penalty for that wrongdoing as possible. On the one hand, as described above, subjects of complaints can be penalized far more heavily than they deserve. On the other, such a system tends to encourage subjects of complaints to deny wrongdoing, making it more difficult for the truth to emerge, for wrongdoers to own their actions, and for complainants to have their genuine grievances addressed.

Outline of a Model Complaints and Discipline System

In the light of this discussion of the functions and general characteristics of a complaints and discipline system, we are now in a position to provide a model complaints and discipline system, which includes the content of the system as well as the processes that may be put in place to achieve its functions. The content of the system will specify such things as: the purposes of the system, who can bring complaints, what kinds of behaviours they can (and cannot) complain about, who can adjudicate complaints, and what kinds of responses are available to those who do adjudicate. Processes include: information about complaints and discipline systems, procedures for making of complaints, filtering and classification of complaints, initial responses to complaints, assistance to complainants and subjects of complaints, adjudication of complaints, enforcement of sanctions, publicizing of findings.

1 LaDuke, S., 'The Effects of Professional Discipline on Nurses', *The American Journal of Nursing*, vol. 100, no. 6, June 2000, pp. 26–33.

2 LaDuke, S., 'The Effects of Professional Discipline on Nurses', *The American Journal of Nursing*, vol. 100, no. 6, June 2000, pp. 32–33.

Information

Information should be freely available to members of the public, and of the relevant occupational group, about how to lodge a complaint, the ways in which complaints will be handled, as well as an explanation of the purpose, structure and workings of the complaints and discipline system. (The development of the internet has obviously facilitated the promulgation of this information and made the lodging of complaints much easier.) Such information may explain:

(1) What is the purpose of the complaint and discipline process?

- Resolution of disputes between practitioners and clients, or between practitioners and their fellows;
- Detection of improper, incompetent conduct;
- Guidance to further professional development as needed;
- Guidance to members of the occupation as to expected standards;
- Sanctioning in the case of serious misconduct.

(2) Who may lodge a complaint?

- Members of the public (clients, consumers);
- Fellow practitioners;
- Professional body (e.g. in case of adverse legal finding).

(3) What cannot be complained about?

(Probably) not

- Complaints about contractual or legal matters;
- Obtaining financial restitution or compensation.

(Although there may be advice about where to go to deal with these, e.g. an alternative dispute mechanism such as a community justice centre, mediation or arbitration or through direct court action.)

(4) What can be complained about?

Distinguish complaints into three kinds (see the discussion of these in Chapter 1):

- *Ethical* – e.g. failure to disclose conflict of interest, bullying of client or employees, misrepresentation of qualifications and expertise, criminality, corruption etc.
- *Technical* – e.g. practitioner failed to use methods and techniques that

would be considered adequate by a competent peer, did not conform to relevant laws and regulations etc.

- *Economic* – e.g. excessive charges, breach of fee protocol.

Perhaps further distinguish:

- *Unsatisfactory professional conduct*, involving a substantial or consistent failure to reach reasonable standards of competence or diligence.
- *Professional ethical misconduct*, involving more serious breaches of occupational standards such as deliberate wrongdoing, including corruption and criminality, or negligent or reckless breaches of occupational standards that the member should have known were likely to create substantial risks of harm or cost to others.

Processing of Complaints

On receipt of a complaint:

- Complainant may be required to provide further information.
- Determination of (lack of) prima facie case (complaint may be rejected as, for instance, frivolous, vexatious, misconceived or beyond the powers of the disciplinary body).
- Complaints judged outside the system's scope may be referred on.
- If it is decided that there is a prima facie case to be answered, complaint is classified (as, for instance, unsatisfactory professional conduct, or professional ethical misconduct).
- Notification of subject of complaint of the nature of complaint, possible courses of action and all other relevant information within (say) three days of receipt of complaint, together with offer of support and advice.
- Response to complainant of determination regarding whether there is a prima facie case to be answered, possible courses of action and all other relevant information within (say) three days of receipt of complaint, together with offer of support and advice.
- Staged, flexible process for resolution of complaint, including exploration of mediation and other means.

Panel Hearing

If a complaint cannot be otherwise resolved, it should go to an adjudicative panel hearing.

- The panel should be independent, impartial, objective and credible. The composition of the panel should be determined with regard to the nature of the complaint; for instance, does it concern a matter where technical judgment will be necessary? Typically, panel members will be drawn from the occupational body as well as other stakeholder groups, such as consumers.

- The laws of evidence do not apply (although natural justice must be observed). The panel must be 'comfortably satisfied' that improper conduct has occurred, based on the evidence presented.
- There is a presumption in favour of open hearings, given the desirability of transparency. The panel may decide to close hearings in particular cases.
- It is not desirable for lawyers to represent parties to a dispute in hearing, given the need for expediency and economy. However, a respondent may be allowed to employ a legal representative who may attend but may not speak during a hearing unless invited by the Chair of the Panel and to the extent of issues defined by the Chair.

Outcome

If the panel decides that the complaint is upheld it may impose sanctions including:

- a fine;
- counselling;
- reprimand;
- admonition;
- the undertaking of specified professional development;
- the obligation for specified decisions to be referred from time to time to an appropriate person;
- the obligation to operate professionally for a specified time under the supervision of an appropriate person;
- expulsion from membership;
- suspension from membership;
- suspension or withdrawal of certification to practice, where this is within the power of the panel.

The complainant and subject of complaint will be notified of the findings within (say) three days.

Appeal

- Grounds for appeal should be specified.
- If complainant, subject of complaint, or member of the professional body is dissatisfied with the finding or sanction imposed by the panel, and there is grounds for an appeal, they should be able to appeal to an independent review panel.
- Membership of the review panel should be different to that of the panel,

although the criteria for membership should be the same.

Publication

- Where a complaint has been upheld, findings should be published (online), in an easily accessible form.
- In the case of serious misconduct, names should be named.
- In other cases, findings should be anonymized.

Analysis, Review and Revision

Data should be gathered about:

- source, number and kind of complaints (for instance, complaints of serious misconduct, professional incompetence);
- response to complaints (for instance, referral to panel, dismissal of complaint as trivial);
- outcomes of complaints referred to panel (for instance, numbers upheld/dismissed, most commonly upheld kinds of complaints, action taken in response to upheld complaints).

These data can be used for such purposes as:

- public education programmes (where, for example, common complaints demonstrate ignorance of relevant law);
- professional education (where common complaints demonstrate lack of competence among membership, common failures of communication to clients etc.).

The peer review complaints and discipline system itself should be reviewed from time to time, with, for example, information gathered from complainants and respondents, as well as from other members of the occupational group, and other clients. Such review may indicate the desirability of revision of parts of the system.

The Duty to Disclose

We each have a moral duty not to harm others. Sometimes, however, our duty goes beyond this: we are obliged not only not to harm others, but to actively assist them. Consider a walker in a park who sees someone having what appears to be a heart attack, where there is no-one else around. Surely we all think that the walker ought to try to help, or at least summon assistance, in this situation. Situations such as this, where we are confident that someone has a duty to assist, have the following characteristics:

- one person has the capacity to help a second;
- the second will probably suffer serious harm if that help is not provided;
- the first person is the only, or the best placed, person who can help the second;
- the cost of helping is not unduly high.

One way in which we can assist others is by disclosing information in our possession about harms they are likely to suffer. Here, we focus on the disclosure of information by a member of an occupation gained in the course of their work. In virtue of their expertise and location, such people are often well placed – and in some cases uniquely placed – to discover and report information about actual and potential unethical behaviour by other individuals or organizations. Of course, all organizations have internal reporting requirements, and these might allow for, or even require, the disclosure of such information. Ethical problems arise in cases when there is no provision for reporting this kind of information, or attempts to report it are resisted or suppressed, or where no action is taken in the face of apparently serious problems.

The following case study illustrates some of the common ethical issues raised by such situations.

Case Study – Bristol Royal Infirmary[3]

Dr Stephen Bolsin moved from London to take up an appointment as consultant cardiac anaesthetist at the Bristol Royal Infirmary in 1988. A good deal of his work was with the hospital's paediatric cardiac surgery (PCS) unit. The first operation he was involved in with this unit at Bristol took all day and evening – in his experience in London, it would have been completed in a few hours. Dr Bolsin was disturbed by this, since length of time is one of the risk factors for an operation. This initial unfavourable impression was confirmed as time went on, with Bolsin becoming convinced that there were unusually high mortality rates associated with heart valve repair surgery. However, as he became aware, there were no reliable statistics kept on the performance of the paediatric cardiac surgery unit. Bolsin began to gather his own data, data that showed that the mortality rate for PCS on children less than one year old at Bristol to be double the national average.

3 This case study is mainly based on *Final Report: Learning from Bristol: the report of the public inquiry into children's heart surgery at the Bristol Royal Infirmary 1984–1995* Command Paper: CM 5207 http://www.bristol-inquiry.org.uk/index.htm (last accessed 20 June 2009); Whittingham, R.B., *Preventing Corporate Accidents: An Ethical Approach*, London: Butterworth-Heinemann, 2008, pp. 323–330; and Davies, M., *Medical Self-regulation*, Aldershot: Ashgate, 2006, pp. 122–142.

To understand the problems Bolsin subsequently encountered in his attempts to have the hospital acknowledge and act on the problems these figures pointed to, it is necessary to have some grasp of the institutional setting he was working within. In the 1980s, the British National Health Service had felt the effects of the prevailing Thatcherite neo-liberal emphasis on improving efficiency and effectiveness in public sector organizations. Two of the consequent organizational reforms were particularly relevant to the events at Bristol. First, certain types of medical procedures were only to be provided at a small number of hospitals, designated as specialized supra-regional services (SRSs), funded centrally on the basis of number of procedures carried out. Loss of SRS status would thus have serious implications both financially and in terms of prestige. Second, a new management structure in hospitals was introduced. Doctors were to be more involved in the day-to-day management of the hospital, through the appointment of 'clinical directors' who were consultants leading the hospital's doctors. The two major posts within the hospital became that of the medical director (the head clinical director), who had responsibility for clinical care, as well as for allocating doctor's workloads and resource allocation, and the general manager, with responsibility for the other activities of the hospital. The general manager was Dr Roylance. As he testified at a subsequent inquiry, he believed that healthcare in the hospital was: 'led by consultants', and that they were 'self-teaching' and 'self-correcting'. On his account it was 'impossible' for managers to interfere. The Bristol clinicians thus operated without any systematic external oversight of the quality of their work: the role of the medical director in setting standards for medical care became all important. As it happened, that role at Bristol was filled by Mr James Wisheart, who was also associate director of cardiac surgery from 1990 to 1992 (at which point the position was taken over by Dr Dhasmana). Although there was an increasing use of clinical audits in this period, at Bristol the prevailing ethos remained that quality of care was purely a matter of professional judgement, and that audits were to be used only for the purposes of professional development.

There was no clear route within the hospital for Bolsin to follow to have his concerns addressed. The Department of Health had advised that clinicians should, in the first instance, take worries about colleagues to senior medical staff in their workplace occupying three designated positions – the so-called 'Three Wise Men' procedure. The very person whose behaviour was of most concern to Bolsin, Mr Wisheart, occupied two of the designated 'wise men' positions, in his roles as Medical Director and Chair of the Hospital Medical Committee. Unsurprisingly, Bolsin did not avail himself of this procedure.

From 1990, Bolsin spent two years trying to move the hospital's management to take action. He began by writing to the general manager of the hospital, as well as to the head of the district health authority, to which the hospital was accountable. In response to his letter, Dr Bolsin was summonsed to the office of the medical director (Mr Wisheart) and (according to Bolsin) rebuked for involving outsiders in the affairs of the hospital. After further agitation within the hospital – and escalating threats to his continuing employment – in 1992 Bolsin took his concerns to Dr Phillip Hammond, who as well as being a doctor, was medical columnist for the *Daily Express* newspaper. He also contributed to *Private Eye* magazine, which published a series of articles detailing the PCS mortality rates at Bristol. At this time Bolsin also contacted the Department of Health, who were reluctant to intervene in what they saw as a dispute between doctors. However, by 1995, the hospital's board had become sufficiently alarmed to set up an independent inquiry. That inquiry led, in turn, to an in 1997 inquiry by the General Medical Council, the national statutory body in charge of doctor's registration, which found Wisheart and Roylance guilty of failing to respond to concerns about the standard of heart operations performed on children, and struck them off the medical register.

Finally, in 1998, the Ministry of Health undertook its own inquiry. In effect, that inquiry became as much an investigation into the systemic problems in regulating the medical profession as into the specific events at Bristol. The report of the inquiry was 540 pages long. Finding that 39 children had died as a consequence of substandard care at Bristol, it made a host of sweeping recommendations for new arrangements for the training and monitoring of medical staff, and for giving the public a stronger voice in their medical care.

The Health Secretary said that the report suggested that, 'Dr Bolsin should be owed a debt of gratitude by the nation'. However, by that time such a debt could only have been paid at a distance: unable to progress his career in Britain, in 1996 Bolsin took a position in Australia, where he still lives. Debates about the appropriateness of Bolsin's actions continued in medical journals, even after the findings of the various inquiries.[4]

Whistle-blowing

In taking his concerns about the unsatisfactory paediatric cardiac surgery procedures at Bristol outside official channels, Stephen Bolsin became a 'whistle-blower'. Here we provide a brief outline of the concept of whistle-blowing, before looking at some of the moral issues it raises.[5]

4 In a letter to the *British Medical Journal*, Rachael Dawson, Senior House Officer at The Queen Elizabeth Hospital suggested that 'discreet inquiries and perhaps an invitation for Drs. Wisheart and Dhasmana to go on a sabbatical to a centre with higher survival figures (if comparable), long before the problem got out of hand, would have been the best answer for both sinned against and sinners.' Cited in Frais, A., 'Whistleblowing Heroes – Boon or Burden?' *Bulletin of Medical Ethics*, no. 170, August 2001, pp. 13–17; for a highly sceptical account of the value of Bolsin's actions and their aftermath, see Fitzpatrick, M., 'After Bristol: the Humbling of the Medical Profession' *Spiked*, 16 August 2001 http://www.spiked-online.com/Articles/00000002D1F4.htm (accessed 3 July 2009).

5 An earlier version of some of the material in this section appeared in Miller, S., Roberts, P., and Spence, E., *Corruption and Anti-Corruption*, Saddle River, NJ: Prentice Hall, 2005, Chapter 8.

A 'whistle-blower', as the term has come to be used, denotes a person who:

- is a member or former member of an organization;
- voluntarily discloses information about possible or actual seriously immoral, corrupt or criminal behaviour;
- provides that information as a matter of public record (through, for example, reports to a media outlet, book publications, revelations before a Parliamentary or Congressional Committee, material placed on a website, etc.);
- identifies themselves as the source of that information;
- provides the information with the intention that doing so will contribute to cessation of the seriously immoral, corrupt or criminal behaviour described and/or make good the damage caused by it.

This characterization allows us to distinguish between whistle-blowers and others who draw attention to bad behaviour. First, the need for institutional affiliation means that people who reveal facts about bad behaviour in private life will not count as whistle-blowers; nor will people who make disclosures about activities in an organization to which they do not belong. So, Phillip Hammond, who published articles in the in the press based on the information he gained from Stephen Bolsin was not a whistle-blower (and investigative journalists and consumer advocates generally are not whistle-blowers in virtue of their activities in uncovering corporate malfeasance, for example). Second, the requirement that disclosure be voluntary means that, for example, witnesses in a court case or official inquiry who have a legal duty to tell the truth are not thereby whistle-blowers. Third, the requirement that the whistle-blower identify his or herself as the source of the disclosure, allows us to distinguish between whistle-blowing and 'leaking', where someone anonymously transmits information that points to wrongdoing. Finally, the fact that the whistle-blower must intend their disclosure to be efficacious in preventing further harm and/or making good the harm already done by the behaviour they reveal means that someone who reveals information about, say, corrupt behaviour that they knew about or were involved in as a matter of historical record, or in order to 'spice up' their autobiography, is not a whistle-blower.

The location of whistle-blowers within an organization means that they are often well placed to identify and reveal serious wrongdoing. In virtue of his medical role, for example, Stephen Bolsin, was able to bring to light problems at Bristol Royal Infirmary that might otherwise have remained undetected. But the institutional affiliation of whistle-blowers also makes whistle-blowing a morally complex and practically fraught activity. The person who thinks that serious wrongdoing – at least short of serious criminality – is occurring in an organization to which they belong must try to address their concerns within that organization, in the first instance, before taking them further. In so doing, they may discover that their suspicions were actually ill-founded. Most importantly, internal disclosure may be sufficient for the wrongdoing to be acknowledged and dealt with. Moreover, failure to make use of internal avenues will raise suspicion that the person who does disclose apparently bad behaviour is driven by such disreputable motives as malice or publicity-seeking. (Stephen Bolsin did, of course, attempt to have his concerns addressed within the hospital over a number of years.)

If, however, no adequate response is made after internal avenues of reporting are used – or if there are no such avenues – the person who believes they have identified serious wrongdoing within an organization to which they belong is faced with the question of what else they should do. One option, of course, is to do nothing. There are usually considerations in favour of this option. Some of these considerations, such as inertia or a misplaced sense of loyalty, should be dismissed. But others are more substantial. To disclose is, in effect, to accuse others – often colleagues – of wrongdoing. The mere fact of accusation itself may have serious ramifications for the accused, even if it eventually turns out to be ill-founded. Moreover, the accuser might fear possible costs to themselves as a consequence of making the accusation, at least if their identity is revealed (we discuss the validity of these fears below). In the face of these considerations it is perhaps not surprising that it appears that more than half of those who observe what they consider to be unethical or illegal behaviour in their workplace, do nothing.[6]

The person who does not want to be passive in the face of what they perceive as serious organizational wrongdoing and who sees no realistic possibility of the organization itself addressing the problem, has at least two options available to them. They can 'leak' – pass information surreptitiously to a third party, such as the press or a regulatory authority, which is likely to act in a way that causes the problem to be addressed. Or they can 'blow the whistle'. The defining difference between leaking and whistle-blowing is that person who leaks retains their anonymity, while the whistle-blower identifies themselves. Leaking has the advantage relative to whistle-blowing that retaining the veil of anonymity avoids, or at least reduces, the potential costs to the discloser. On the other hand, it will often diminish the effectiveness of the disclosure, since the accusation cannot be reinforced by the credentials of the accuser, and the anonymity of the accusation is likely to foster the suspicion that it is made out of vindictiveness or for some other disreputable reason. So leaking is likely to be less personally costly than whistle-blowing, but also less effective.

The Costs of Whistle-blowing

There is now a good deal of empirical evidence indicating that whistle-blowing does tend to be personally highly costly. These costs can include counter-accusations, and attacks on the whistle-blower's credibility, loss of employment, and loss of opportunities for future employment, with consequent damage to the

6 Rothschild, J., and Miethe, T.D., 'Whistle-Blower Disclosures and Management Retaliation', *Work and Occupations*, vol. 26, no. 1, 1999, pp. 107–128.

whistle-blower's financial and emotional well-being, the stability of their personal relationships and their health.[7] Even with the introduction of 'whistle-blower protection' legislation in many jurisdictions, the lot of the whistle-blower tends to be dire. While such legislation may make it less likely that the whistle-blower will be directly dismissed or demoted by their own organization as a consequence of their whistle-blowing, it is much harder to prevent other, less formal, sanctions – such as ostracism, denial of promotion, and the like – both by the organization against which the original complaint was made, and by other similar organizations. Rothschild and Miethe's 1999 survey of whistle-blowers found that 64 percent had effectively been 'blacklisted' from getting another job in their field.[8] Stephen's Bolsin's inability to continue his medical career in the UK was, then, typical of the experience of whistle-blowers.

The retaliation that whistle-blowers suffer for their actions stems from the contest for legitimacy that the whistle-blower's complaint creates.[9] That complaint can never be simply about the particular bad behaviour that occasions it (such as the inadequacy in the surgical procedures at Bristol). It is also pointing to – at best – a failure by the organization to identify and respond to that behaviour, or an attempt to hide it, or at worst an active complicity in it.

At the moment the whistle-blower makes their accusation, their credibility and moral status and that of the organization or group they are accusing thus become negatively correlated: to the extent to which the whistle-blower is seen as a truthful, well-motivated person then the organization must be seen as having failed to function properly and to put in place proper accountability mechanisms. Understanding the relationship between whistle-blower and organization in terms of a contest for legitimacy also helps to explain the common experience of whistle-blowers of having their personal credibility and motivation attacked – of being 'smeared' – by the organizations they complain about. Such smear tactics, if effective, deny the whistle-blower legitimacy in the eyes of the world and remove the need for the organization to address, let alone redress, the behaviour that is the subject of the whistle-blower's complaint. The more serious the accusation made by the whistle-blower, the more serious the retaliation against them – including attempts to discredit them – tends to be. Rothschild and Miethe found that in almost every case, whistle-blowers had not anticipated the retaliation they experienced.

---

7 A study into the effects of whistle-blowing on individual whistle-blowers found that in seven of the 35 cases examined long-term relationships broke up. There were 77 children of subjects, and 60 of them 'were adversely affected'. Lennane, K.J., '"Whistleblowing": a Health Issue', *British Medical Journal*, 307, 1993, pp. 667–670.

8 Rothschild, J., and Miethe, T.D., 'Whistle-Blower Disclosures and Management Retaliation', *Work and Occupations*, vol. 26, no. 1, 1999, pp. 107–128.

9 Sawyer, K., Johnson, J., and Holub, M. 'The Necessary Illegitimacy of the Whistleblower', http://papers.ssrn.com/sol3/papers.cfm?abstract_id=917316 (accessed 4 June 2009).

Surprised as they may be by the response of the organizations against which they complained, whistle-blowers are likely to be even more taken aback by the lack of support they receive from the agencies that they might turn to for support, such as regulators and occupational associations. Again, to understand this lack of support we need to look at what the truth of claims made by whistle-blowers would say about these agencies – that they are failing in carrying out the tasks that are central to their reason for being. The whistle-blower can be seen by regulators as a competitor, rather than an ally. This is especially likely to be so in cases like that of Stephen Bolsin, where the activity of the whistle-blower threatens the status quo of an occupation or profession which is (largely) self-regulating.

The competition for legitimacy between whistle-blowers and their targets, combined with the lack of responsiveness of regulatory bodies, also helps explain the apparent obsessiveness of many whistle-blowers and their frequent recourse to the media. Since both the professional standing and personal welfare of the whistle-blower is contingent on their being able to establish their credibility, it is not surprising that whistle-blowing becomes what Rothschild and Miethe call their 'master status ... the critical bedrock of one's identity'.[10] Given the importance of establishing their bona fides and the frequent lack of effective support from regulators and occupational bodies, it is also not surprising that whistle-blowers often take their case to the media.

These two common characteristics of whistle-blowers in turn lend support to various psychological explanations of whistle-blowers: as moral zealots and rule-worshippers, with no tolerance for the necessary compromises and moral ambiguity of real life; as publicity seekers and malcontents; or as paranoid, 'professional victims'. The Australian Federal Ombudsman, Ron McLeod, had this to say about whistle-blowers:

> At times, whistleblowers do not help the process by resorting to personal abuse when a problem may be systemic rather than personal. They may make threats, which unfortunately all too often lead to threats being made in response. They can be protective against any insult or offence to themselves, but make wild and sweepingly offensive statements about others. They demand proof at a higher level than they are prepared to offer. They can seem narrowly focused on a particular issue, or even obsessed by it. But then they expand the field of discussion, whether they're winning or losing on the initial point. They can be impractical and politically or socially naive; they fail too often to recognize that a small win is a win nonetheless and not just the first concession in what they believe will be a continuing process.[11]

---

10 Rothschild, J., and Miethe, T.D., 'Whistle-Blower Disclosures and Management Retaliation', *Work and Occupations*, vol. 26, no. 1, 1999.

11 McLeod, R., *Blowing the Official Whistle*. Address by Ron McLeod AM, Commonwealth Ombudsman, to Transparency International Whistleblowing Symposium,

In fact, empirical research has revealed no significant correlation between personality type and likelihood of whistle-blowing: situational factors are of much greater predictive value. As Miethe and Rothschild note:

> ... contrary to popular images of whistleblowers, objective requirements of specific roles or jobs that employees find themselves in, coupled with employee's perceptions of the ethics, openness, and democracy of their employing organisation, have much more influence over the propensity to blow the whistle than do psychological or dispositional characteristics.[12]

Reducing the Cost of, and Need for, Disclosure

As we pointed out above, people often gain information about wrongdoing by virtue of their occupational location and expertise, and there is at least a prima facie duty that they make such wrongdoing known. It is now common for professional associations to include duties to disclose knowledge of wrongdoing in their codes of ethics. The Code of Ethics of the Safety Institute of Australia,[13] the peak body for occupational health and safety professionals, for example, advises what a professional member should do if they 'become aware of an organization breaching Occupational Health and Safety legislation or standards resulting in risk of injury or disease.' In the first instance, they should try to have the organization acknowledge and rectify the problem, but if 'there is no action on the part of the organization and the only way of reducing the risk is to disclose their knowledge to a third party, they should do so'. Similarly, many occupational codes of ethics require members to report colleagues whose actions they regard as seriously harmful or illegal.

As discussed above, however, there may be real costs consequent on reporting. One of the conditions we enumerated for the existence of a duty to assist (of which the duty to report is a specific instance) is that the cost of helping is not unduly high. The bar for this condition is no doubt higher for members of an occupational group than it is for ordinary members of the public, given the collective duty of the group to act to realize the defining purposes of the occupation. Could it however be so high that a person could be required to act in a way that they know is likely to expose them to public attempts to discredit them and to the possibility of the end, or at least a drastic restriction, of their career and to the undermining

---

Sydney, August 2002. In his address, McLeod did go on to outline the organizational dimensions of whistle-blowing.

12 Rothschild, J., and Miethe, T.D., 'Disclosing Misconduct in Work Organizations: An Empirical Analysis of the Situational Factors that Foster Whistleblowing', *Research in the Sociology of Work*, vol. 8, 1999, pp. 211–227.

13 *Victorian Code of Ethics and Minimum Service Standards for Professional Members of OHS Associations* http://www.sia.org.au/about/ethics/ (accessed 5 July 2009).

of their personal relationships? There are two possible plausible responses to this question. In situations where there is potentially high personal cost of disclosure it might be held that there is no duty to disclose: those who nevertheless do disclose will be seen as moral heroes, acting above and beyond the call of duty, while those who do not will be justified in not doing so. On the other hand, in situations where failure to disclose might allow ongoing harm to others of the most grievous kind to occur, as in the Bristol case, it might be held that there is a duty to disclose, even where doing so might be personally costly. In such cases, nevertheless, it obviously becomes understandable that those with such a duty will find it impossible to live up to it, given its costs: their failure is excusable, even if not justified.

As we argued in Chapter 2, members of an occupation as a group can have a collective duty to act in ways that realize the defining ends of the occupation, and as individuals have duties that stem from this collective duty. The duty to disclose, where it exists, is such a duty. We have been pointing to the problems with the claim that this duty exists, or that it will be effective, in cases where disclosure is likely to be very costly. The situation in which members of an occupation are aware of or involved in a high level of wrongdoing, but deterred from disclosing, is clearly extremely morally problematic. In broad terms there are two possible responses to such situations: to lessen the need for disclosure, by reducing the opportunities and attractiveness of wrongdoing; and to lessen the potential costs of disclosure when it is nevertheless desirable. Indeed, one way of reducing the likelihood of wrongdoing is by lessening the cost of disclosure. The more likely it is that disclosures will be acted on, and the less likely it is that those who make them will be penalized, the more likely it is that they will be made. And the more likely it is that they will be made and acted on, the greater their deterrent value, so the less attractive wrongdoing becomes.

Occupational groups can reduce the costs of disclosure through, for example, supporting and guiding whistle-blowers. Moreover, since the need for whistle-blowing reduces as effective internal and external accountability mechanisms are put in place, occupational groups should press for such mechanisms. However, as discussed in Chapter 2, and has been demonstrated in cases such as the Bristol Infirmary scandal, there are problems in ensuring that members of occupations will make disclosures about colleagues, particularly where it is members of the occupation themselves who are charged with investigating and taking action. One way to deal with these problems is to make reporting serious misconduct legally mandatory. The Australian state of New South Wales, for example, included the following provisions in the NSW Medical Practice Act 2008:

> (1). A registered medical practitioner commits reportable misconduct in the following circumstances:
>
> (a) if he or she practises medicine while intoxicated by drugs (whether lawfully or unlawfully administered) or alcohol;

> (b) if he or she practises medicine in a manner that constitutes a flagrant departure from accepted standards of professional practice or competence and risks harm to some other person;
> (c) if he or she engages in sexual misconduct in connection with the practice of medicine.
>
> (2). A registered medical practitioner who believes, or ought reasonably to believe, that some other registered medical practitioner has committed reportable misconduct must, as soon as practicable, report the conduct to the Board.

The institution of such mandatory reporting has a number of advantages, relative to a regime of voluntary reporting. First, it changes the cost-benefit calculation to be made by a doctor contemplating disclosure. Obviously, it makes disclosure more attractive, by imposing a potential cost for non-disclosure. At the same time, it decreases the likely costs of disclosure. Allegations of disreputable motivation are much less likely to be made, or to stick, where it is clear that failure to disclose would be imprudent as well as immoral. Moreover, since disclosure will set in train a legal process, the legitimacy of the discloser will be established by the law, rather than through a contest with a powerful organization.

Chapter 5
Ethical Reputation Indexes and Ethics Audits

It is agreed on all sides, that the global financial crisis taking place at the time of writing is the worst since the Great Depression. The main aspects of the problem are frozen credit markets, the sub-prime mortgage crisis and an impending global recession. The crisis has involved major corporate investment and mortgage banking collapses and bailouts in the US (Lehmans, Freddie Mac and Fannie Mae), UK (Northern Rock), Europe (Fortis, Hypo) and it is having a devastating effect on home owners who cannot pay their mortgages (foreclosures), retirees whose pension funds have plummeted in value, employees whose jobs are at risk in the imminent recession, and taxpayers who money is being injected into the banking system in vast quantities to rescue it (e.g. $700 billion by the US government).

Unethical, including imprudent, practices have been identified as being among the principal causes of the crisis. These practices include: (i) reckless and predatory lending by banks; (ii) the selling of toxic financial products, notably non-transparent packaged bundles of mortgages (including sub-prime mortgages), designed by 'creative' lawyers (amongst others) to circumvent regulatory barriers; (iii) failure to avoid or adequately manage structural conflicts of interest, including ratings agencies assessing the non-transparent toxic financial products mentioned above as high quality because the investment banks that packaged them – and who fund the ratings agencies – allegedly had good risk assessment processes; (iv) massive frauds, e.g. Bernard Madoff's ponzi scheme; (v) excessive executive remuneration that, in numerous cases, has in effect rewarded management failure, e.g. in the case of the failed investment banks and the giant insurer, AIG. However, the current financial problems share important features with recent, as well as not so recent corporate collapses and scandals. Recall the corporate scandals of the 1980s in the US and elsewhere: the stock market crash, a junk bond collapse, the bankruptcy of numerous highly-leveraged clients, the prevalence of the unlawful practice of insider trading, and the fining and imprisonment of the likes of Michael Milken and Ivan Boesky. And what of the collapse of Enron, Worldcom, One Tel, HIH circa 2001? These had a devastating effect on shareholders, employees and others. Moreover, they involved a range of unethical practices such as conflicts of interests, auditing failures, and corrupt (if not unlawful) practices, e.g. Enron's Special Purpose Entities (SPEs) calculated to mislead shareholders in relation to actual performance.

We have argued throughout this book that laws and regulations are not sufficient to curb ethical misconduct and promote ethical attitudes. There are a number of reasons for this, including the following: (a) laws and regulation inevitably play 'catch up' in relation to new and emerging ethical problems (including loopholes that are exploited by 'creative' accountants and 'legal engineers'); (b) it is both impractical and undesirable for all ethical standards and virtues to be embodied in laws and regulations – aspirational ethical goals are a case in point, and; (c) ethical behaviour and attitudes cannot simply be regulated into existence. But if laws and regulations are not sufficient, what other factors can play a role? We suggest that a key element in the establishment of effective integrity systems for at least some occupational groups, including occupational groups in the financial sector, is the mobilization of professional reputation.

Professional Reputation

A good professional reputation is much sought after by members of occupations, perhaps especially by members of the traditional professions, and a poor one is to be avoided at all costs. Accordingly, there is an opportunity to mobilize this reputational desire in the service of promoting ethical standards. Here the aim is to ensure that professional reputation aligns with actual ethical practice, i.e. that a group or individual's good or bad reputation is deserved. The way to achieve this is by designing appropriate integrity systems. Key elements of an integrity system track compliance with rules, e.g. accountability. The additional thought here is that key elements of an integrity system should track features of occupational groups that determine or should determine reputation. Most explicitly, a reputational index could be constructed whereby an ethics audit awards scores in relation to specific ethico-professional standards.[1]

Deserved reputation represents an important nexus between self-interest and concern about others, and so for our purposes here, between the self-interest of occupational groups and concern about consumers, clients or the public generally. Here there are three elements in play: (i) reputation; (ii) self-interest; and (iii) ethical requirements, such as particular ethico-professional standards, but also more general desiderata such as client/consumer protection. The idea is that these three elements need to interlock in what might be called a virtuous triangle.

First, reputation is linked to self-interest; this is obviously already the case – individuals, groups and organizations desire high reputation and benefit materially and in other ways from it. Second, reputation needs to be linked to ethics in that reputation ought to be deserved; as already mentioned, the integrity systems are the means to achieve this. Third, and as a consequence of the two already-mentioned links, self-interest is linked to ethics: given robust integrity systems that mobilize

1 Earlier versions of some of the material in this section and in the following two sections appeared in Alexandra, A., Campbell, T., Cocking, D., Miller, S., and White, K., *Professionalisation, Ethics and Integrity Systems: The Promotion of Professional Ethical Standards, and the Protection of Clients and Consumers*, Sydney: Professional Standards Council, 2006; and Miller, S., *The Moral Foundations of Social Institutions: A Philosophical Study*, New York: Cambridge University Press, 2009, Chapter 6.

reputational concerns, it is in the self-interest of individuals, groups and firms to comply with ethico-professional standards. We should also reassert that we do not believe that self-interest is the only or ultimate motivation for human action; the desire to do the right thing is also a powerful motivator for many, if not all people. Accordingly, the triangle is further strengthened by the motivation to do right.

In recent years, the notion of a Reputation Index has gained currency in a number of contexts, especially in business and academic circles. The term seems to have a number of different senses. Sometimes it is used to describe a way of measuring the reputation that an organization actually has. Since reputation exists, so to speak, in the eye of the beholder, actual reputation does not always match deserved reputation. Accordingly, sometimes the term is used to describe a way of calculating the performance of an organization on the basis of which its reputation should be founded.

The first step in the process is to determine a way of accurately measuring the ethical performance of individual or organizational members of occupational and industry groups; this is an ethics audit.

Here, we stress the importance of *objective* measures of ethical performance. The latter might include such things as: results of consumer satisfaction surveys; gross numbers of warranted complaints and trends thereof; numbers of disciplinary matters and their outcomes; outcomes of financial, and health and safety audits (e.g. regarding electronic crime and corruption vulnerabilities). It would also include the existence of institutional processes established to ensure compliance with ethico-professional standards, e.g. codes of ethics and conduct, financial and other audit processes, ethics committees, complaints and disciplinary systems, fraud and ethics units, professional development programmes in ethics, ethics officers. Notwithstanding the in-principle existence of objective measures of ethical performance, there is a general problem in this area that we discuss below (in the section on performance measures, reputation and distortion).

In addition to the ethics audit itself, there is a need for a process that engages with ethical reputation. Since ethical reputation should reflect the findings of the ethics audit, an ethical reputation audit should drive the relationship between de facto ethical performance (in effect, the deserved reputation) and actual reputation for ethical performance. The way to achieve this is by the participation of as many occupational and industry players as possible in ethics audits, and by the widespread promulgation of the results of their de facto ethical performance (as determined by the ethics audit), including in the media. Naturally, the results promulgated could be more or less detailed; they could, for example, simply consist of an overall rating as opposed to a complete description of the ethics audit results.

Lack of participation is obviously problematic for reputational indexes; without widespread participation, reputation cannot be mobilized. What means are available to ensure the participation of occupational groups and organizations in reputational indexes? (Of course, in the case of those indices that simply measure compliance with legal requirements, there is no need to secure 'participation'; the compliance failure is already in the public domain and reputational indexes simply provide additional and more targeted publicity.) In relation to the problem of non-participation, there is a variety of responses ranging from the mandatory use of reputational indexes by members of professional or industry groups (on pain of exclusion from the relevant professional or industry association) through to the provision of various kinds of incentive. The Professional Standards Council in Australia provides one kind of example for occupational groups. It offers capped liability as an incentive to occupational groups to participate in its ethico-professional standards schemes.

Another problem is effectiveness. The use of reputational indexes can easily be reduced to 'tick-the-box' processes on the part of clever, well-resourced organizations seeking to avoid actual compliance with ethical standards in favour of engaging in elaborate exercises in window-dressing. Hence the need for meaningful ethical audits conducted by independent, adequately resourced, and professionally trained, ethics auditors.

Professionalization, Reputation and the Professional Standards Council

The increased need for more effective integrity systems for occupations is twofold. First, there is the need to rehabilitate the traditional professions, such as law, that are now increasingly practised in new settings – in particular, in large multi-disciplinary corporate organizations. Second, there is the need to refine and raise ethical standards in emerging professions, e.g. journalists, social workers, or (more generally) in occupations simply seeking to professionalize in the sense of articulating and embedding ethical standards as part of a broader process of raising their standards and status.

Organizations such as the Professional Standards Council (PSC) in Australia are important participants in this process of ethico-professionalization; indeed arguably this is the raison d'être of the PSC. Moreover, the conferring of good reputation is central to the PSC's role.

The PSC offers capped liability to occupational groups in exchange for their establishment of integrity systems; accordingly, there is a financial incentive to occupational groups to join a scheme and, thereby, reduce their insurance premiums. However, the PSC also offers a kind of ethical accreditation to occupational groups via its *Cover of Excellence* scheme; groups establishing an appropriate integrity system are awarded a Cover of Excellence. Indeed, arguably the central instrument of the PSC in its effort to promote ethico-professional standards is not so much the capped liability provision, but rather its de facto ethical accreditation of occupational groups – an accreditation that confers good ethico-professional reputation on these groups.

As we saw above, having a good reputation can be made to depend primarily on possession of an effective integrity system, because an effective integrity system is one that maintains and promotes compliance with high ethico-professional standards and, therefore, provides an assurance that a good reputation is deserved. Accordingly, the PSC has an important role: to establish and reinforce the dependence between good reputation and possession of an effective integrity system.

This is, in effect, what the PSC is doing by approving its *Cover of Excellence* schemes for those occupational associations that have put in place appropriate integrity systems – or, at least, significant components of integrity systems, e.g. complaints and discipline processes.

Moreover, the PSC, and like organizations, could do more to strengthen this dependence between good reputation and possession of an effective integrity system, by mobilizing the desire on the part of occupational groups to gain a high reputation – and avoid a low reputation. For example, an integrity system that includes reputational indices for members of an occupational group, and corresponding ethics audits, directly connects the desire for a high reputation on the part of a member of an occupational group to the maintenance and promotion of ethico-professional standards. To this extent the integrity system in question is more effective than it would otherwise have been.

Naturally, this whole process is predicated on the reputation of occupational groups and firms actually being *deserved*. Good reputation that is *undeserved* is not an ethical good; it does not benefit consumers or clients, and it does not serve the public interest. It is also important to stress that the credibility of the PSC is also on the line: its approval of a *Cover of Excellence* scheme must be seen to be warranted.

Integrity systems for different groups may vary in the weight they give certain considerations over others. So, for instance, anti-competitive concerns or claims to professional autonomy with respect to a body of knowledge may be more relevant to some groups than others. Accordingly, deserved reputation will track such differences. It will, for instance, be more significant to the overall deserved good reputation of, say, a real estate agent, to establish that she does well in relation to anti-competitive and market norms than it will be for most doctors. That is, such an integrity system provides the reputational indices against which reputation may be assessed and so 'good' reputation may be shown to be deserved or otherwise.

The PSC's instruments aimed at enhancing integrity systems for occupations, and which provide such reputational indices, are:

- the development of effective codes of ethics, conduct or practice, in collaboration with occupational associations;
- complaints and discipline procedures; and
- professional development and ethical education programmes.

As we have noted, a significant and common finding from the empirical study we conducted for the PSC was that having or improving an ethico-professional reputation was a key driver across various occupational groups, and correspondingly for seeking *Cover of Excellence* accreditation from the PSC. To this extent it supplemented – and perhaps, in some cases, even replaced – the incentive to occupational groups provided by liability capping.

This is not so surprising. The provision of affordable insurance for certain professionals, such as lawyers and accountants will, of course, remain important and 'capping' may reasonably be expected to remain a necessary as part of a suite of mechanisms to address the need for affordable insurance. However, for many occupational groups, such as real estate agents, access to affordable insurance (indemnity cover) is not an important need that must be met to be able to continue to practise and provide their services to the community.

Ethical Reputation Indexes

If reputation is to be mobilized in the service of raising ethical standards then the following steps need to be taken. First, for each occupation it needs to be determined what the appropriate ethical standards are. Second, an integrity system for these ethical standards needs to be developed that comprises various elements, e.g. a complaints and discipline process. Third, indices need to be worked out in relation to such integrity systems and their workings, e.g. the number of complaints. Fourth, an applicable reputational index (comprised in part of a set of appropriate indices) needs to be developed and accepted by a reasonably large cross-section of the occupational group in question. Fifth, an independent entity needs to be established to conduct the actual process of assessing members of the occupational group in question (i.e. applying the reputational index). Sixth, the results need to be made public.

Reputational indexes can be developed and used to measure a variety of different kinds of entity. Thus, members of an occupational group can be rated as a whole or against one another; firms in a given industry can be rated as a whole or against one another. Here we note that what is made publicly available is not necessarily a ranking of members of an occupational group or set of organizations. Rather, there could be simply the statement that the minimum threshold of ethical standards had been met, e.g. by way of a Cover of Excellence 'badge'. Alternatively, there might be, say, a five star ratings system, in which more than one practitioner or firm could get a five star rating. And there are other possible systems.

There are important differences between occupational groups that need to be reflected in integrity systems and hence reputational indexes. The reputation of the lawyer or engineer may be measured against how well they exercise their substantial and discrete technical (and related ethical) expertise and skill. However, technical (and related ethical) expertise is not so much a feature of an occupational area, such as real estate agents: accordingly, reputation would not be so dependent upon such criteria.

Again, reputation for the traditional professions (in so far as it is concerned with relations with the public) can be in part characterized in terms of the exercise of distinctive professional responsibilities and duty of care concerning their clients. On the other hand, the reputation of commercially focused occupations, such as real estate agents, can be in part characterized in terms of the realization of appropriate commercial goals, albeit in the context of a commitment to consumer protection.

Naturally, there are some ethical standards that hold for all occupational groups, e.g. avoidance of theft, fraud. Some hold for all occupational groups but vary to some extent in their characteristics or seriousness from one occupation to another, e.g. conflicts of interest. Some of these standards concern the workings of the market, such as:

- In what ways is the occupation or association committed to market regulation that is aimed at providing fair competition?
- To what extent is there fair competition in the field?
- How might fair competition be promoted?

As we use the term here, an 'Ethical Reputation Index' (ERI) is, in the first instance, a way of accurately measuring the ethical performance of individual or organizational members of occupational groupings, which we call an Ethical Audit. Here, we stress the importance of *objective* measures of ethical performance, including gross numbers of warranted complaints, and compliance with institutional processes established to ensure compliance with ethico-professional standards. However, an effective ERI should be more than simply an accurate gauge of ethical performance. Since ethical reputation should reflect the findings of the Ethical Audit, an ERI should also function to align actual with deserved reputation through the accessible presentation and promulgation of the results of the ethics audit. So understood, an effective ERI will consist of the following elements:

1. An occupation-specific composite ethical performance index, consisting of a number of discrete dimensions of ethical performance both at the micro-level, such as, for example, honesty, respect for confidentiality, avoidance of conflicts of interest, etc. (and perhaps relative weightings for these different dimensions) and at the macro-level, such as, for example, possession of a detailed and enforced code of conduct, tailored and well-functioning complaints and discipline system, and an appropriate and mandatory professional development programme.
2. Measurable ethical performance indicators for each dimension, for example upheld complaints, institutional processes of ethics assurance (again, there may be a number of weighted indicators for a single dimension, to enable an overall performance score in that dimension).
3. Mechanisms for gathering data relevant to the performance indicators (such as, for example, logged complaints, findings of disciplinary proceedings,

results of self-assessment, surveys of consumer satisfaction, etc.).

4. Methods for aggregating and analysing gathered data. (Elements 1–4 jointly constitute the Ethical Audit component of the Ethical Reputation Index.)
5. Presentation of findings of the Ethical Audit in accessible and meaningful form. (One issue here is the use of comparative versus absolute performance measures – should, for example, a practitioner be rated as 'in the top tenth percentile' in some dimension, or 'having a score of 0.62' in that dimension, or both? Another issue concerns 'raw' versus 'adjusted' data. For instance, if a practitioner works in a high-risk area, should the number of complaints against them be presented in bare numerical form, and/or in comparison with the average number, or should they be presented in a form weighted to take into account the difference between practice environments?)
6. Promulgation of the findings of the Ethical Audit in a manner that is likely to reach relevant stakeholder groups (e.g. through occupational and consumer group publications and online forums).

A well-functioning ERI aligns actual with deserved reputation. In so doing it provides a number of benefits for both the members of an occupational group, and their clients/customers. For clients, it protects them against unethical treatment and reduces 'transaction costs' by enabling them to enter into a relationship with a professional without having to take elaborate precautions against unethical behaviour. For already ethically well-motivated professionals, it provides assurance that their behaviour will be recognized and rewarded. For those who are not already so well-motivated, it provides an extra incentive to act in an ethically appropriate manner, while reducing the benefits to be gained from the promotion of their (undeserved) public reputation through advertising, media appearances etc. An ERI thus can both encourage ethical behaviour and lead to an economically more rational allocation of resources.

Finally, we note that there are a variety of possible ERIs and that different ERI types might be appropriate for different occupational groups; indeed, there might be some occupational groups in relation to which no ERI is either necessary or desirable. One possibility is that ERIs are, generally speaking, more appropriate for market-based occupations than traditional professions or, at least, more appropriate for less heavily regulated occupational groups.

Performance Measures, Reputation and Distortion

Notwithstanding the potential of reputational indexes (in the context of holistic integrity systems) to mobilize reputation in the service of raising ethical standards, the use of such indexes is problematic in a number of respects. We have already noted some of these above; for instance, the objectivity of measures, insufficient participation and the need for independent adjudication to avoid conflicts of interests. (We discuss conflicts of interest in greater detail in the following section.)

However, the general problem of providing objective measures of performance needs to be looked at in more detail and, in particular, in relation to untoward unintended consequences.

Here, we can consider this problem in an area in which sophisticated measures of performance have been in use for a considerable period of time, namely, the provision of health care.

The performance of individual surgeons and hospitals in the USA, the United Kingdom and elsewhere have been subjected to detailed testing, e.g. surgeons' report cards,[2] and the results published so as to provide guidance to would-be patients. Indeed, patient knowledge of the past performance of surgeons in terms of the number of failed versus successful operations relative to the type of patient (for instance, in terms of being in a high risk category) has been suggested to be within the purview of the patient's right to be fully informed, i.e. a matter of informed consent.[3]

Whatever the scope of the right of informed consent in relation to a surgeon's past performance, it is evident that clients and customers have a general right to knowledge in relation to ethical misconduct, including misconduct above and beyond criminality. However, such a right falls far short of a right to knowledge of objective measures of overall ethical performance. Accordingly, the justification for the latter is in terms of the resulting good outcomes and these depend, in turn, on the possibility of objective measures and the absence of untoward unintended consequences from the publication of such measured ethical performance.

According to Hibbard, Stockard and Tusler, publishing data concerning the quality of care in hospitals significantly improves the quality of such care, in the clinical area in particular, and does so in part as a consequence of concerns regarding their public image on the part of the hospitals in question.[4] More specifically, hospitals provided with a public report were found to be more likely to be engaged in improving their performance than those provided with confidential reports. Moreover, surveys of consumers conducted two months after the publication of reports indicated that consumers were likely to have changed their ranking of different hospitals based on the results of these reports.

Doubtless, there is a variety of motivations in play here including, but not restricted to, the desire to avoid reputational loss and to acquire reputational gain. For instance, some hospitals might be concerned with the quality of health care that they provide just for its own sake, and measuring their performance might reveal areas of weakness to them and, thereby, causes them to lift their game.

2 Clarke, S., and Oakley, J., 'Informed Consent and Surgeons' Performance', *Journal of Medicine and Philosophy*, vol. 29, no. 1, 2004, pp. 11–35.

3 Clarke, S., and Oakley, J., 'Informed Consent and Surgeons' Performance', *Journal of Medicine and Philosophy*, vol. 29, no. 1, 2004, pp. 11–35.

4 Hibbard, J., Stockard, J., and Tusler, M., 'Hospital Performance Reports: Impact on Quality, Market Share and Reputation', *Health Affairs*, vol. 24, no. 4, 2005, pp. 1150–1160.

Moreover, the concern with reputation can itself stem from different motives; it might be that some public hospitals are concerned with reputation for its own sake, while others, for instance, private hospitals, are only concerned with the impact of reputational gains and losses on their market share. In fact, it is plausible that any given hospital will have mixed motives, with some motives stronger in the case of some hospitals than others.

While the efficacy of performance measures in health care might be demonstrable, at least in some areas and with respect to some measures, it is not without pitfalls, as various commentators have pointed out.[5] Thus, measurement of performance is subject to gaming by those being evaluated, it can produce distortions and it does not obviate the need for unquantifiable judgement. Such 'gaming' has included falsifying data, e.g. changing the response times of ambulances to emergencies. In relation to distortion, the publication of surgeons' report cards has in some cases evidently discouraged surgeons from operating on the sickest patients. More generally, if performance is measured in terms of X then resources may well be reallocated so as to ensure that high measures of performance in terms of X are achieved and, as a consequence, other areas or aspects of performance that are not well measured by X may well be under-resourced.

Speaking generally, the performance of professionals, especially their 'ethical' performance, cannot be evaluated purely by recourse to quantifiable measures; the complexity and subtlety of the activities in question resist such quantification. Thus, a complaints and discipline system might look highly efficient and effective in purely quantitative terms in that all complaints are investigated and all appeals looked at, but the actual quality of the investigations and adjudications in relation to very important matters might be quite poor; investigations and adjudications of complex matters do not lend themselves to wholly quantifiable forms of evaluation. This is not to say that there is no place for quantification and measurement, but rather that inevitably there is a need for judgement.

Conflicts of Interest

A fundamental ethical standard of particular relevance to professional reputation is the avoidance or management of conflicts of interest. Conflicts of interest are, of course, a potent source of ethical misconduct, indeed of corruption. Moreover, conflicts of interest are often not well-understood; this is so, at least in part, because determining whether or not something is a conflict of interest can be a difficult matter in need of sustained ethical analysis. Finally, and most importantly for our concerns here, conflicts of interest are intimately connected to questions of professional reputation. So much so that the avoidance of even the *appearance* of a conflict of interest can be an ethical requirement; it can be an ethical requirement

5 See, for example, the editorial in the *International Journal for Quality in Healthcare*, vol. 19, no. 4, 2007, pp. 183–186.

by virtue of the damage it can do to the reputation of a practitioner, firm or even an entire occupational group. Consider the reputational damage done to auditors when they appear to have a conflict of interest in undertaking well-remunerated consultative work for the very firms that they audit.

A conflict of interest occurs when a person or group's personal interest comes into conflict with their occupational duties, or when a person or group has two occupational roles, and the duties of one compete with the duties of the other.[6] For example, if a member of the tax office decided to adjudicate his own tax return, he would have a conflict between his personal self-interest and his fiduciary duty. Again, if an accountant also happened to be the manager of a football club, and as an accountant she was asked to audit the club's financial statements, she would have a conflict of interest.

Conflicts of interest are conducive to ethical misconduct in a variety of ways, depending on the nature of the role of the person or group that has the conflict of interest. For example, a magistrate or police officer with a conflict of interest may fail to apply the law impartially, or a businessman who is a member of a local government body might vote to award himself a contract.

Sometimes it is hard to determine whether an apparent conflict of interest is real or not. And theoretically, a conflict of interest that is only apparent might not be problematic. However, often even the *appearance* of impropriety can be harmful to the reputations of persons and groups, and to the confidence that people need to have in practitioners and the occupations and institutions to which they belong. Accordingly, it is often very important to clarify and resolve apparent conflicts of interest, as well as to avoid real ones. Indeed, it may well be important to avoid even the appearance of a conflict of interest.

Further, the precise nature and boundaries of occupational roles should be clearly delineated and rendered perspicuous, for if this is not done then role confusion can arise, and with it the possibility of real or apparent conflicts of interest.

Before we proceed further, let us determine what is a *conflict of interest*. According to the 'standard view':[7]

> A conflict of interest is a situation in which some person *P* (whether an individual or corporate body) has a conflict of interest. *P* has a conflict of interest if and only if (1) *P* is in a relationship with another requiring *P* to exercise judgement on the other's behalf and (2) *P* has a (special) interest tending to interfere with the proper exercise of judgement in that relationship. The crucial terms in this definition are 'relationship', 'judgement', 'interest' and 'proper exercise'.

6 An earlier version of some of the material in this section appeared in Miller, S., Roberts, P., and Spence, E., *Corruption and Anti-corruption*, Saddle River, NJ: Prentice Hall, 2005, Chapter 8.

7 The 'standard view' is provided by Davies, M., *Encyclopedia of Applied Ethics*, Academic Press, 1998, Volume 1, A–D, p. 590.

The 'relationship' required must involve one person trusting (or at least being entitled to trust) another to exercise judgement on his behalf. 'Judgement' is the ability to make certain kinds of correct and reliable decisions that require knowledge or skill. 'Interest' is any influence, loyalty, concern, emotion, or other feature of a situation tending to make *P*'s judgement (in that situation) less reliable than it ought to be. What constitutes a 'proper exercise' of judgement is usually a matter of social fact; it includes what people ordinarily expect, what *P* or the group to which *P* belongs invites others to expect, and what relevant laws, professional codes, or other regulations require.[8]

What is generally wrong with a conflict of interest is that it renders one's judgement less reliable than it should be, and results in a failure to discharge one's duty properly.

Generally, a conflict of interest can arise in at least one of two ways:

1. Person A has a self-regarding interest that is in conflict, at least potentially, with his or her occupational duty, and therefore this has the tendency to interfere with the proper exercise of A's judgement with regard to that duty.
2. Person A has two potentially competing occupational duties or roles that are in conflict with each other, at least potentially, and therefore one duty or role has the tendency to interfere with the proper exercise of A's judgement with regard to the other duty or role.

For example, there is a clear conflict of interest in the case of an accountant, Joe, who audits the financial statements of a club, and who is also the manager of that club. Consider the interest in the club that Joe has as the manager. Joe *qua* manager has an interest in maintaining the image of the club as financially viable. Now consider Joe's interest as an auditor in providing a true and fair statement of the club's financial situation. Joe's interest as a manager in maintaining the image of the club might have a tendency to make his judgement as auditor less reliable than it should be. Clearly there is a potential conflict of interest here, and one that arises from these two conflicting roles.

Crucially for our purposes in this book, conflicts of interest are conducive to ethical misconduct. For example, a police officer who also moonlights for a security firm faces a conflict of interest when called upon to investigate criminal allegations against the manager of the security firm. The police officer's personal interest in keeping his additional job conflicts with the requirements of his role as a police officer, and may interfere with the proper exercise of his judgment in fulfilling his duty, as police officer, of upholding the law. He might be less zealous than he ought in his investigation of the criminal allegations against his boss. Again, a judge who presides over a criminal trial that involves his daughter as the

8 Davies, M., *Encyclopedia of Applied Ethics*, Academic Press, 1998, Volume I, A–D, p. 590.

defendant in a rape case has a conflict of interest. Notice that the police officer in the first case, and the judge in the second case, may in fact not act corruptly; each may well intend to do his duty – by investigating the criminal allegation thoroughly (in the case of the police officer), or conducting the trial fairly (in the case of the judge). However, in each case the conflict of interest remains, and therefore there is at least an *apparent* inability to discharge their role requirements properly.

The above examples illustrate that although not every instance of a conflict of interest necessarily results in wrongdoing, conflicts of interest are nevertheless conducive to wrongdoing. Thus, it is best to avoid conflicts of interest; it is best, for example, that a judge with no familial connections to the defendant is appointed to the trial. In cases in which the conflict of interest is a minor one, and/or could only be avoided with great difficulty, it may be acceptable for the person with the conflict to disclose it without avoiding it. If so, disclosure might need to be backed up by some suitably rigorous process of accountability.

As we have already seen, many conflicts of interest involve a conflict between one's self-interest and the requirements of the role that one occupies. Others involve a conflict between two different roles that one occupies. Still others involve a degree of role confusion, which serves to mask a conflict of interest.

Conflicts of interest involving self-interest are reasonably obvious, but what of *role conflicts*? By way of illustration, consider the following restrictions imposed in some organizations or professions: one cannot be both judge and advocate, or both editor and manager of advertising revenue of a newspaper, or both cashier-banker and manager of accounts payable and receivable in a large corporation. Underlying this institutional division of potentially conflicting roles is the *principle of the division and separation of responsibilities*. This principle is adhered to so that the proper exercise of one's judgement cannot be adversely affected by allowing one to occupy two potentially conflicting roles or functions. The role conflicts involve primarily a conflict between two roles, offices or institutions. Traditionally, a Western democratic state is divided into distinct institutional 'estates', for example, the government and the judiciary, whose functions are by design supposed to remain separate and independent. The separateness and independence of these institutions from one another is designed to ensure a division of power, and also to ensure that potentially harmful conflicts of interest are avoided. Without this 'separation of powers' we would have the intolerable situation in which a senior politician is the judge in a case involving a political opponent or in a case involving an adjudication in relation to the legality of a proposed government policy.

Dealing with Conflicts of Interest

The most obvious way to deal with conflicts of interest that might result in corruption is to avoid them. In cases where there is a potential conflict between an institutional actor's self-interest and the duties of his institutional role, regulations requiring avoidance of these conflicts need to be introduced, and some form of accountability mechanism established.

Role conflicts can best be avoided through a strict division of duties and responsibilities that does not allow one person to occupy both roles. For example, there is a traditional division of accounting responsibilities between the cashiering and banking functions on the one hand, and the accounts payable and receivable functions on the other.

In the case of accountancy firms, conflicts of interest might be avoided through the strict division and separation of the auditing and financial consultancy functions within the firm. However, this control may not be adequate to avoid conflicts of interest if fees from financial consultancy services far exceed auditing fees. One possible solution to this problem is to increase audit fees substantially so that they at least match those from financial consultancy services. If that is not possible, perhaps it should be impermissible for an accounting firm to provide auditing and consultancy services to the same client.

The potential conflict between the requirement for objectivity and impartiality in news reporting and editorial comment, on the one hand, and the commercial demands of advertising, on the other, can be avoided by having a strict division between those two functions in a media organization.

It is not always possible to avoid conflicts of interest. The next best solution is to disclose them. However, disclosure is only acceptable in the case of otherwise ethically acceptable practices. It would not be ethically acceptable for a politician to be a judge. Accordingly, disclosure would not be a solution to that conflict of interest.

On the other hand, the mandatory disclosure of advertorials as being in fact advertisements – and, therefore, in no sense to be regarded as sources of impartial and objective information – might be sufficient to eliminate the pretence that they are anything other than advertisements. In this particular type of conflict of interest, disclosure has almost the same effect as avoidance. For it eliminates the deceptive cloak, and requires the advertorial to be seen for what it is – an advertisement.[9]

As we have seen, some *apparent* conflicts of interest can be as ethically problematic as real ones because of their potential to generate a loss of confidence in institutional processes, or a loss of trust in institutional actors. One way of eliminating these untoward effects of apparent conflicts of interest is disclosure. Often full and frank disclosure reveals that the apparent conflict of interest is not a real conflict of interest, and this is sufficient to satisfy relevant parties that there are no grounds for loss of confidence or trust. Consider, in this connection, full disclosure of all donations to political parties.

---

9 Davis, M., 'Conflict of Interest', *Encyclopedia of Applied Ethics*, Volume I, A–D, 1998, p. 593.

Chapter 6

Empirical Research, Ethics and Occupations

It is evident that research into ethical problems, whether in the area of occupational ethics or in other areas, needs to be firmly grounded in the empirical work of social and natural scientists.

Certainly, ethics pervades the sciences; even the basic goal of science, namely truth, is an ethical notion, and social and natural scientists alike ought to aim at the truth, even if sometimes they produce falsity or self-serving ideology. Nevertheless, the resolution of complex ethical issues, including controversial ones such as limiting green house gas emissions or human enhancement, must first begin with the scientific facts; the starting point for the resolution of such ethical disputes should be the best scientific evidence available. And this goes as much for ethical issues in occupational settings as it does elsewhere.

Research in applied ethics must also rely on the practical experience of practitioners and others. For example, solutions to the problem of corruption in business and the professions depend in large part on the understandings provided by the practitioners themselves. What are the dynamics of corruption? Does corruption begin with minor forms of compromise? Is there a slippery slope from minor misdemeanours to gross forms of corruption? The answer to these empirical questions depends heavily on accessing the actual experience of practitioners; their collaboration with researchers is essential.

Naturally, scientific findings are not in themselves sufficient to guide actions and generate public policy. It may well be a fact that fraud in large corporations is caused by a conjunction of commercial pressures and a psychological propensity to be seduced by money and success. It does not follow from this that we ought to try to control the spread of fraudulent practices: neither does it follow that we ought not. Such policies only follow if we make a further judgement, the judgement that fraud is harmful and morally wrong; not only harmful to profits, but harmful in that it is a species of theft and theft is morally wrong. The latter, however, is a moral judgement. Accordingly, public policy – and reason-based action more generally – necessarily relies not only on scientific facts, but also on moral values.

Moreover, in invoking the distinction between scientific facts and moral values we are not invoking the fact/value distinction, if that distinction is taken to imply that values are not objective features of reality. The statements that Jones is unreliable or that Smith committed the moral offence of theft are, we submit, often statements of objective truth and sometimes known with greater certainty than many scientific propositions, e.g. scientific claims and counter-claims in relation to the origin of the universe. This is why business decisions (the *interests* of shareholders), the adjudications of law courts (X is *guilty* and Y is *innocent*) and public policies (e.g. the *rights* of workers) are routinely made in large part on the basis of such moral claims.

Naturally, the moral values are often only implicit, rather than explicit, in the reasoning that guides the policies or actions. Moreover, the moral values in play may be controversial or idiosyncratic or simply the reflection of the interests of powerful groups within the society. But the point is that inevitably moral values are involved; scientific facts by themselves do not generate actions or policies. And the fact that these moral values may be implicit or idiosyncratic or reflective only of powerful groups within the society is all the more reason to unearth and scrutinize them. Once examined, these assumed values may turn out to be defective; and the policies based on these defective 'values' will be bad policies. It is unacceptable to base important organizational decisions, criminal adjudications or public policy on unproven pseudo-scientific claims. It is equally unacceptable to base such decisions and policies on moral values that have not been identified and subjected to rational scrutiny.

As we hope this book has made manifest, ethical analysis has a central place in occupational ethics. However, in this chapter, our concern is with empirical research in the service of ethical ends. We consider empirical research in relation to the development of integrity systems for occupational groups. In order to focus our discussion, and exemplify the utility of research in this area, we present some of the findings from a recent empirical study that we conducted for the Professional Standards Council in Australia.[1] This research deployed qualitative and quantitative research methods in order to: (i) delineate the main features of the integrity systems operative in a number of occupational groups; (ii) identify some of the key ethical problems confronted by practitioners in these occupations, and; (iii) unearth possible solutions to some of these problems. While the research concerned itself with a number of diverse occupational groups, we will focus here only on three of these, namely engineers, auditors/accountants, and lawyers. Specifically, we will make use of some of the qualitative research undertaken in Australia in the form of in-depth interviews with key informants from the engineering profession, and auditing/accountancy; and some of the findings from the quantitative study that was conducted in relation to the legal profession.

Engineers

Engineering is a well-established profession with a history of guidance by goals that are not primarily commercial but which are primarily oriented towards serving a significant public good, namely public safety. One important development over

---

1 Alexandra, A., Campbell, T., Cocking, D., Miller, S., and White, K., *Professionalisation, Ethics and Integrity Systems: The Promotion of Professional Ethical Standards, and the Protection of Clients and Consumers*, Sydney: Professional Standards Council, 2006.

the past few decades, however, has been the privatization of major government instrumentalities such as electricity commissions, which employed large numbers of engineers and were largely dominated by engineers. Nowadays, engineers most commonly work in organizations whose prime purpose is not engineering – for instance, mining companies or manufacturers. Another significant change has been the increasingly multidisciplinary nature of the work and, therefore, of the skills required of engineers to do such work.

Accordingly, engineers present a good example of a notable traditional profession – that is, one properly guided by commitment to a clear and significant ethical good, which, in light of changes in the nature and circumstances of much of its practice, faces new issues and challenges in retaining and strengthening its ethico-professional direction.

Engineering is a highly significant profession, both in terms of the numbers of practitioners, and in terms of the role they play. Engineers are integrally involved in the shaping of the material environment within which we live – we are all affected every day in myriad ways by the work of engineers.

Engineering is characterized by its orientation to the solution of practical problems in the material world. The extensive range of engineering specializations includes chemical engineering, electronic engineering, civil engineering, geomantic engineering, environmental engineering, and so on. Despite the wide differences in fields of application and specific knowledge and skills of these specializations, all have a common form, containing the following elements:

- engineering science;
- design and development; and
- management and organization.

Jointly, these elements allow for the solution of the practical problems facing engineers.

Engineers Australia, the peak professional body for Australian engineers, categorizes those qualified engineers into three occupational groups:

- 'Engineering Home Occupations' – where, for example, a holder of a Civil Engineering degree works as a civil engineer.
- 'Engineering Related Occupations' – where, for example, the same person works in a position where engineering qualifications and experience are necessary, but where the tasks undertaken are not solely related to those qualifications and experience, such as an engineering manager.
- 'Other Occupations' – members of this category may work in totally non-engineering jobs. In many cases, however, they are working in positions in which they draw on their engineering experience and knowledge, even if they are not directly exercising their engineering skill. Someone who is an executive in a company specializing in engineering equipment, for example, would be so classified.

It is noteworthy that 'Engineering Home Occupations' is the smallest of these categories, with about 34,000 members; while 'Other Occupations' is the largest, with some 133,000 members. In some occupations (such as teaching and nursing) large numbers of qualified practitioners not currently working in the field is evidence of a high rate of attrition, where practitioners have left the occupation for other lines of work. In the case of engineering, however, the disparity between numbers qualified and numbers practising their profession has a quite different significance. As noted above, 'management and organization' is one of the constituent elements of engineering activity. The ability to muster and deploy the resources – including personnel – necessary to overcome a practical problem in an effective and efficient manner is fundamental to what it is to be an engineer. As engineers gain seniority, it is unsurprising that many of them move into managerial positions, which can be seen as extensions of their engineering career, even if these positions do not directly involve the exercise of their specific engineering skills. This hybrid nature of the 'engineer/manager' is especially productive of ethical complexity, as discussed further below.

The bulk of engineers appear to work in organizations whose prime purpose is not engineering (such as mining companies, manufacturers, etc.). In turn, these organizations are either private or public. An important development over the past few decades has been the privatization of major government instrumentalities such as electricity commissions, which employed large numbers of engineers, and were largely dominated by engineers.

A significant change has occurred over the past 30 years in the make-up of consulting engineering firms, and the nature of the work that such firms undertake. Increasingly, consulting engineering firms provide multidisciplinary services, rather than services based on specific engineering specializations. For example, such firms may be employed to manage a project that involves coordinating a whole range of different professions and trades including, but not limited to, different engineering specializations. While this is true across the board, for obvious reasons it is particularly the case in larger firms. Not only does this mean that engineers increasingly engage in multidisciplinary work, but also that they themselves must have multidisciplinary skills. The move towards large, multidisciplinary consulting engineering firms has also had implications for the governance structures, with a trend away from partnerships to corporate structures.

In most jurisdictions in Australia, minimum standards for the delivery of engineering services are not legislated. There are, however, a number of influential professional bodies, notably the peak professional body, Engineers Australia (with about 80,000 members), as well as the Association of Professional Engineers Scientists and Managers of Australia, and the Association of Consulting Engineers of Australia – whose members are firms, not individual practitioners. Engineers can be certified through the National Engineering Registration Board. These bodies have a common Code of Ethics, run Continuing Professional Development (CPD) programmes, and have discipline and complaints processes in place. However, among the engineers we interviewed, there was a good deal of scepticism as to the effectiveness of these programmes and processes. In any case, membership of, or recognition by, such bodies is not mandatory, and many practising engineers are not involved in them.

Our interviews indicated that many engineers appear to feel a strong identification with, and pride in, the professional ethos of engineering. That said, it seems plausible that the most important external influence on engineers' behaviour (especially consulting engineers) is the law rather than, say, professional codes of ethics or complaints and discipline processes. Engineers in such areas as construction, and major projects generally, work in a highly litigious environment, where the effects of an adverse legal ruling can be extremely damaging professionally. On the other hand, since engineers can continue to practice without being members of a professional body, the threat of disciplinary action by such bodies is unlikely to exert a significant deterrent effect in many cases.

There is a paucity of professional ethics training in engineering, at least in Australia, and what education there is does not address the complexities of engineers housed in large organizations and/or in multidisciplinary settings.

In short, the integrity system for engineers in Australia is overly reliant on legal frameworks (as opposed to, say, effective complaints and discipline systems), undeveloped in various ways, e.g. in respect of professional ethics education, and has significant gaps in it, e.g. in the use of reputational indexes. Let us now turn to some of the potential areas of ethical risk.

Ethical Problems for Engineers

Public Interest

It is common for engineers' work to be used by many more people than the original client. Civil engineers, for example, are involved in the design and erection of structures such as bridges, buildings and dams which are used by large numbers of people, other than those who commissioned them. The work of engineers can thus affect members of the public positively, by increasing their amenity and economic opportunity, or negatively, by placing them in danger or by engaging in environmentally or socially destructive projects. There will often be a prima facie conflict between the interests of engineers' clients – in completing a project as cheaply as possible, say, or in finding a solution to a problem that shifts its burden to others – and the interests of the public.

The priority of the public interest is a fundamental tenet of engineering ethics, and of the self-understanding of the engineering profession. The Code of Ethics of Engineers Australia, for example, says: 'Members shall place the responsibility for the welfare, health and safety of the community before their responsibility to sectional or private interests, or to other members'.

However, it is not a straightforward matter to understand how the notion of 'public interest' should be understood here. The Australian Code of Ethics, for instance, does not specify what constitutes the public interest. This leaves ethical issues about the environment and the community at the level of an issue of personal conscience. However, the existence of the tenet at least allows that if engineers invoke it they could expect to be supported by Engineers Australia. Thus, an employee engineer could conceivably take recourse to this tenet in not complying with the demands of an employer. Indeed, a number of the engineers we spoke with indicated that they had appealed to this code – or more broadly, to their professional obligations – when they were under pressure to act in a way that they found unethical.

Furthermore, it is doubtful that engineers have a specific legal duty to act in the public interest. Clearly engineers, like other professionals, have a duty of care not to act in a way that could foreseeably cause direct harm to members of the public. In particular, they become liable if they act in their professional capacity in ways that could predictably compromise the safety of others (through, for example, using a method of construction in building a bridge that had not been rigorously tested), or failing to act to prevent such compromise.[2] They do not have any legal duty to act in ways that create the greatest amount of benefit for the public. It would thus seem that they have no legal duty *not* to engage in a project that has long-term environmentally destructive effects (such as the loss of habitat of a rare species of bird, for example), provided that no individual could predictably suffer the risk of physical injury or material damage.

In a major review of British legal judgments, John Uff, Nash Professor of Engineering Law, Kings College, London, pointed out that: 'The civil law is concerned solely with duties owed by Engineers to individuals or to groups whom the Engineer ought reasonably to contemplate as likely to suffer, particularly in terms of physical injury, as a result of his negligence.' Uff concludes that: '... the law affords no support to a general duty enforceable by or at the suit of the public at large.'[3]

Commercial/Financial Considerations vs. Professional Values

Engineers tend to want to remove risk as far as possible.[4] In organizations with a strong engineering culture, such as the state electricity commissions, this led to the phenomenon of 'gold-plating', with large amounts of redundant capacity built into the system to ensure against failure. Management, on the other hand, tends to want to manage risk, as one among many elements in a decision-making situation.

2 The legal situation regarding duty of care is, evidently, complex. It is particularly complex in relation to engineers. John Uff describes and explores some of these complexities in Uff, J., *Engineering Ethics: Do Engineers Owe Duties to the Public?* London: Royal Academy of Engineering, 2002, esp. pp. 9–12.

3 Uff, J., *Engineering Ethics: Do Engineers Owe Duties to the Public?* London: Royal Academy of Engineering, 2002, p. 12

4 Our discussion in this section is largely based on our discussions with engineers.

There is obvious potential, then, for professional values to come into conflict with organizational goals, including commercial success and financial viability. Perhaps the most well-known and spectacular example of this was the space shuttle Challenger disaster, in which engineers prioritized organizational goals ('think like a manager not an engineer' one was told) over safety considerations, with disastrous consequences, including the death of the astronauts.[5] Furthermore, such conflict can occur not only between engineers and others, but also personally. Many areas of consulting engineering, for instance, are highly competitive, with pressure on the engineer either to cut corners in their own work in order to be able to win tenders and make a profit, or to acquiesce in the dubious practices of their clients.

Commercial pressures have always created tensions with true professional independence for consulting engineers. Commonly, for example, one engagement by a client has the potential to lead on to further work for the same client. If, for example, an engineer produces a report that indicates that a project favoured by a client is unviable on the grounds of cost or safety, he makes it less likely that he will get to work on that project. A number of recent developments have made it even more difficult for engineers to act autonomously. In an era of electronic communication, for instance, clients can start interacting with engineers on a report earlier and more easily, and thus influence its direction to a greater extent than was previously the case.

The privatization of major government instrumentalities such as electricity commissions over the past couple of decades has had a significant, if indirect, effect on the engineering professions. Such instrumentalities employed large numbers of engineers but, more importantly, fostered a very strong engineering culture, focusing on safety and thoroughness, and insulated to a large extent from commercial pressures. They thus generated and reinforced norms that pervaded the rest of the engineering community.

Government practice in recent years has also contributed to raising the commercial pressures on consulting engineers. In the past, governments would typically commission a large practice to prepare a report on, for example, environmental impact of some proposed significant development, or on future transport needs. Now they are more likely to commission a number of different firms to prepare reports on different elements of the proposed project. This makes it easier for government employees to 'guide' the direction the various reports take, and for government not to accept reports that lead to politically unpalatable conclusions. Since the reporting engineers are bound by normal contractual conditions, they have no right to make the contents or treatment of such reports public, short of drawing attention to illegality or immediate danger to the public.

---

5 For an influential discussion of a famous case in which this tension between engineering and managerial approaches came to the fore see Davis, M., 'Thinking Like an Engineer: The Place of a Code of Ethics in the Practice of a Profession', *Philosophy and Public Affairs*, vol. 20, 1991, pp. 150–167.

Accountants and Auditors

Auditing and accountancy are also well-established traditional professions and are notably characterized by an important economic function and significant ethical ideal, namely to provide honest and accurate financial reporting. Accountants, and particularly auditors, however, have come under intense pressure with respect to their standards, competence and integrity primarily due to their perceived role in failing to prevent or predict some catastrophic corporate collapses in recent times, e.g. Enron and the collapse of Arthur Andersen. As a consequence, the profession, particularly the auditing sector, is under considerable scrutiny and is anxious to improve its reputation and re-secure the trust without which it cannot effectively perform its important economic functions. In auditing, reputation is all; once an auditing firm loses its credibility as a competent, independent source of the financial health of companies it is finished, as the spectacular collapse of Arthur Andersen demonstrated.

Accountants in Australia, the United Kingdom, the United States and elsewhere have developed, over many years, systems of internal self-regulation, which are now subordinate to an extensive legal framework within a complex and changing co-regulatory regime. The current regulatory scheme in Australia, which is best described as co-regulation, is a complex intertwining of internal and external mechanisms in which statutory and common law effectively legalize the professional standards set (and largely enforced) by independent professional accounting bodies cooperating with each other and various regulatory agencies, such as the Financial Reporting Council (FRC) and the Australian Securities and Investment Commission (ASIC). It is also important to note that, while accountants must obtain accreditation through statutory bodies in order to practice in certain fields, such as auditing and taxation, and cannot join professional bodies without obtaining educational standards accredited by these bodies, there are no formal monopolies or licensing requirements that apply to accounting practice as such.

In Australia, accountants in public practice outside the four major accounting firms participate in a scheme with the Professional Standards Council, under which they benefit from capped liability if they meet the professional standard requirements of the PSC, e.g. operate a complaints and discipline system, have a code of ethics and a professional development programme. Approximately 10,000 of the 38,000 accountants who are members of the three professional bodies in NSW participate in a PSC *Cover of Excellence* scheme. In general, the members of professional associations participating in the schemes have no problem in meeting the formal requirements for schemes agreed between the accounting bodies and the PSC, as the key ingredients were already in place. In practice, problems arise only over details, such as matters relating to annual reports to the PSC (for example, trouble obtaining the insurance claims data required by the scheme). At the margin, participant membership in a *Cover of Excellence* scheme involves little more than a small additional annual fee. The PSC, therefore, plays a fairly small part in an overall regulatory set up that is highly developed relative to most other occupational groups.

Nevertheless, accountants and, particularly, auditors have come under intense pressure with respect to their standards, competence and integrity due to their perceived role in failing to prevent or predict the catastrophic corporate collapses (Enron, Parmalet, WorldCom, HIH) that were related, in various ways and to varying degrees, to 'creative accounting' with respect to financial reporting and persistent undetected fraudulent financial conduct. The profession, particularly the auditing sector, is therefore under considerable scrutiny and is anxious to improve its reputation and re-secure consumer trust – without which it cannot effectively perform its important economic functions. It thus has a strong interest in the reputation aspects of *Cover of Excellence* schemes as part of a wider public rehabilitation exercise.

Accountancy practice may be broken down into five main areas: accounting, auditing, taxation, management consulting and financial management services – all of which give rise to different ethical problems and insurance needs. Accountancy firms have developed the scope of their activities, from financial accounting and auditing to a broad range of consultancy services, to meet the demands for professional business advice and assistance. While large firms have introduced technical, legal, and operational management separation between their auditing and consultancy organizations, close relationships between these two sectors of their business remain.

Further, while accountants have always worked for and within businesses as well as in accounting firms, it is now also common for accountants to be employed or involved in multi-occupational firms providing a range of services to businesses. These developments are often identified as part of the explanation for lapses in accounting ethics, due to increased commercial pressure and a diluted professional culture.

The professional status of accounting is firmly rooted in its knowledge base which has, in some areas, reached such a degree of technicality as to be unintelligible outside (and sometimes within) professional accountancy circles. The expertise required by the two principal professional bodies (Institute of Chartered Accountants in Australia (ICAA) and the Certified Practising Accountants (CPA)) requires at least an undergraduate degree accredited by them, followed by a post-graduate qualification and several years of mentored practice. While anyone may practice as an accountant, membership of one of the three professional bodies (the third being the National Institute of Accounting (NIA)) is a de facto prerequisite for career enhancement, thus enabling these bodies to exercise significant influence over their members through continuing education, codes of ethics, and complaints and disciplinary proceedings.

Accountants are subject to the rules of their professional body and to the requirements of regulatory authorities established by statute. Company auditors and insolvency practitioners must register with the Australian Securities and Investment Commission (ASIC), and tax agents must register with the Tax Agents

Board in their state (there is a proposed nationwide registration scheme), which requires meeting certain educational and experience criteria.

The Financial Reporting Council (FRC), a statutory body under the ASIC Act as amended by the *Corporate Law Economic Reform Program (Audit Reform and Corporate Disclosure) Act 2004*, oversees the process for setting accounting and auditing standards that have legal backing from 1 July 2006, and monitoring the effectiveness of the audit independence requirements.

CPA Australia and ICAA have a very detailed joint Code of Ethics for Professional Accountants, prepared by the Accounting Professional and Ethical Standards Board (APESB), which came into effect on 1 July 2006. The main change is to the requirement that a member in public practice, who has been asked to replace an existing accountant, must have direct communication with the existing accountant in respect to audit engagements, with member discretion in respect to other engagements.

Recent company law reform gives legal status to parts of the joint Code. All three associations have complaints procedures requiring complaints to be in writing. Complaints may be investigated by a committee consisting of experienced members, whose findings may be forwarded to a disciplinary committee, which involves non-members, with a range of sanctions available including additional hours of professional development, fines and loss of membership. Its findings are published without the complainant's name and often without the name of the accountant in question (depending on the seriousness of the complaint).

Membership of the Accountants Scheme (for CPAA and ICAA members) or the very similar National Institute of Accountants Scheme (for NIA members) is open on a voluntary basis to members of the professional associations on the payment of a fee.

Such members must confirm that they have complied with the requirements of the scheme and must comply with its various requirements, such as holding professional insurance to the limit of the insurance cap, and are subject to the complaints and discipline systems of the associations with respect to these matters. In addition to the standard requirements of the schemes, the associations accept that the legally binding arrangements are designed to create 'a culture of excellence and responsibility'.

Evidently, accountants and auditors have long-standing integrity systems that are well developed in many respects, including codes of ethics (and codes of practice), complaints and discipline systems, and professional development programmes. In addition, reputation – as opposed to professional or legal sanctions – is a powerful driver. On the other hand, at least in Australian jurisdictions, reputation has not been mobilized to the extent that it might; namely, in the context of a comprehensive integrity system replete with reputational indexes, ethics audits and the use of research tools.

Ethical Problems for Accountants

Ethical issues identified by interviewees in Australia and that are also prominent in the international literature include the following.

Competition

With only four big accounting firms operating in Australia, there is a lack of genuine competition – which is evident in fee setting practice. However, there are many 'second tier' large firms.

Currently, the professional codes do point out how crucial accurate and honest accounting is to a market economy, but much more could be made of the role of accountancy in providing the basis for open and fair competition in business generally, and the accounting profession in the role of guardians whose task is in part to counter the anti-competitive aspects of much business practice. Attention could be given to competition between accountants and accounting firms in their codes of ethics. Currently there is reference to promoting 'fair dealing', 'improper use of confidential information', misleading advertising of accounting services and dealing with misleading information issued by business clients. However, the ambivalent attitude to competition between accountants is revealed in Section 240.1 of the Code of Ethics of Professional Accountants, which states: 'The fact that one member in Public Practice may quote a fee lower than another is not in itself unethical'.[6] This is in the context of a concern that low fees leads to a dilution of technical and professional standards. This could amount to a market failure (due to the fact that accounting and auditing inadequacies do not become evident unless the business concerned becomes insolvent) or a failure of markets (in that auditing, for instance, is not the sort of activity that should be subject to market forces), but it also raises the question of improper professional self-interest.

Both government and – publicly at least – the major accounting bodies favour amalgamation to bring the accounting profession under one professional association, which would enable the profession to speak with one voice. Whatever its merits on other grounds, this can be viewed as a threat to open competition. This might be countered by an increased emphasis on competition ethics.

Auditors' Independence

Audits are a small and decreasing percentage of revenue of large accountancy firms that have moved primarily into providing consultancy services to business, often the same business for which they carry out audits. Hence, there is a good

6 Accounting Professional and Ethical Standards Board (APESB), 'Compiled APES 110 Code of Ethics for Accountants' (February 2008), sec. 240.1, p. 25. The Code of Ethics is available at http://www.apesb.org.au/standards.php?id=10 (last accessed 14 September 2009).

deal of competitive pressure, which often results in low-priced audits that may not be well carried out:

(a) since they are part of a larger package or services, and
(b) used as a hook to lead to more consultancy work.

From a survey by the NIA of 700 accountants who are members of PSC (to which only 120 responded) other threats to auditor independence are apparent:

(a) over-dependence of some accountants on small number of clients;
(b) being simultaneously company secretary and auditor;
(c) 20% had a minor problem with self-auditing – the accountant being both auditor and the person who prepared the financial statement in a self-managed superannuation fund.

The survey also identified:

(a) 31%: no letter of engagement (hence disputes over payment of fees);
(b) 7.5%: no professional indemnity insurance;
(c) 10%: trust accounts not audited;
(d) 2.8%: not a registered tax agent, but doing tax.

This has been the subject of intense scrutiny and some legal reform in Australia, arising from the Ramsay Review of 'The Independence of Australian Company Auditors' (October 2001), a review by the Federal Parliament's Joint Standing Committee on Public Accounts and Audit (JSCPAA 2002), the Royal Commission following the collapse of HIH (2003), and a Treasury review under the Corporate Law Economic Reform Program (CLERP 9, 2002) which led to the *Corporate Law Economic Reform Program (Audit Reform and Corporate Disclosure) Act 2003* (Cth).

It is noteworthy that the very recently introduced new legal requirements relate to auditing and its interconnections with other accounting services, the principal ones being:

- a requirement for the rotation of individual auditors after 5 years;
- a legal obligation to follow the auditing standards established by the Auditing and Assurance Board (from 1 July 2006); and
- a specification of types of conflict of interest that totally compromise auditor independence and whose violation may now constitute a criminal offence.

Nevertheless, it is generally accepted that it is impossible to 'legislate for independence' through 'inflexible rules' and that auditor independence is, in part, 'a state of mind' – which means that considerable regulatory oversight remains channelled through the professional bodies and their codes of ethics, which now go into fine detail as to what constitutes a failure of audit independence, and what individual accountants and their firms ought to do about it. This is only partly because professional judgement is still required, as auditing is based on simple testing and internal control reviews due to the impossibility of checking every transaction.

It is therefore clear, even at this early stage, that the move towards more law within the co-regulatory scheme will still be heavily dependent on the internal codes, their enforcement, the culture of professional bodies and their members, and a development of the existing auditing processes that are carried out by the professional bodies with respect to their members' activities.

Fraud

This was illustrated by cases of senior people in auditing firms colluding with the auditees; and coercion within a firm not to disclose (and/or to fall in with) dubious practices.

More attention could be paid to developing a professional culture where whistle-blowing is more accepted within professional bodies and is therefore a reasonable alternative for accountants who become aware of fraudulent accounting.

A related problem is that of an 'expectation gap' as to the reliability of audits – which could be addressed by increased transparency as to the scope of financial reports and audits.

Moreover, auditors are not necessarily experts in fraud detection, particularly sophisticated forms of fraud performed by offenders who are themselves knowledgeable in relation to auditing practices.

In this and other areas of ethical concern, the increasing emphasis placed on auditing practices by professional bodies should be encouraged and, where possible, go beyond processes and standards to examine the substance of accounting transactions.

Commercial Pressure

Occasionally, pressure can lead to creative but 'strictly legal' accounting where financial reporting is significantly misleading for audit users. This is exacerbated by the tendency of professionals to resist routinization of their knowledge base, including resistance to specific rules.

According to *Professional Conduct Tribunal of Institute of Chartered Accountants* data there are about 350 complaints per year, with 40–50 referred to tribunal complaints about fees, failure to do tax returns, insolvency complaints, and failure to comply with technical accounting/auditing standards. In general, there appears to be a perception of commercial pressure undermining ethical professional standards.

The accounting profession exemplifies the need for a powerful professional ethic. In particular, its role in auditing and advising business requires that its operations are trustworthy. Indeed, credibility is a prerequisite of an accountant's market value. Accountants therefore have a considerable collective interest in their ethical reputation – yet the business temptations to serve the client who is paying for the services sets up an almost inevitable and unavoidable conflict of interest between the profession's 'responsibility to act in the public interest' and its need to survive within a competitive market economy.

In these circumstances, clear and firm legal obligations are required – but this has to be supplemented by an ethic that is not only committed to obeying the law (in spirit as well as letter), but in promoting norms that cannot be captured entirely within legal rules and which go beyond the legal minimum that it is possible to require. Bill Edge, Australian Auditing and Assurance Standards Board Chairman put the matter this way: 'Regulation alone will not regain public trust. Confidence in the capital markets depends on confidence that the reporting and regulatory process will deliver accountability and transparency. This in turn depends on integrity – and integrity depends on one's core ethical beliefs and behaviours.'[7] However, this goes against the grain of a great deal of accounting practice and advice, which can be seen as taking clients as close to profitable illegalities as is feasible.

Solicitors

Here, we discuss a quantitative study of solicitors functioning in incorporated and multidisciplinary legal practices in NSW. The focus of this study was the complaints data and the self-assessment process implemented by the Office of the Legal Services Commissioner as part of the regulation of these entities.[8]

The detailed quantitative study of solicitors yields some important trends in relation to ethical problems confronted by that group. Useful means for reversing some of these trends, such as the self-assessment instrument used by the Office of the Legal Services Commissioner, and the deployment of intelligence-driven practices, such as profiling unethical practitioners and firms on the basis of aggregated complaints data, are explored.

Traditionally, in NSW and, indeed, Australia, solicitors practised as sole practitioners or in partnership with other legal practitioners. However, while sole

---

7 Campbell, T., and Houghton, K. (eds), *Ethics and Auditing*, Canberra: ANU E Press, 2005, p. xiv.

8 The material in this section was originally prepared by Seumas Miller and Mathew Ward for Miller, S. and Ward, M., *Complaints and Self-Assessment Data Analysis in Relation to Incorporated Legal Practices*, Report for the Office of the Legal Services Commissioner, 2006, pp. 1–45, relying in part on the input of Steve Mark and Molly Hutcherson for the NSW Office of the Legal Services Commissioner.

practitioner and partnerships remain the most prevalent form of legal practice in NSW, the *Legal Profession Act 2004* also allows legal practitioners to practise as members of multidisciplinary partnerships ('MDPs') involving legal service providers who are not legal practitioners – for example tax experts who are not solicitors – or as officers or employees of incorporated legal practices ('ILPs'), which may also be multidisciplinary.

There are currently over 600 ILPs in NSW, of which over 90 are multidisciplinary practices. This number is increasing at the rate of approximately 25 per month and it is anticipated that, by 2010, ILPs on the NSW model will be the preferred structure for the provision of legal services – not just in NSW, but in Australia generally.

As recently as 2004, NSW was the only jurisdiction in the common law world to allow for the incorporation of legal practices *including* multidisciplinary incorporated practices. All other Australian states and territories have since followed or are about to follow suit.[9] Moreover, a number of recent developments, including the Australian Commissioner for Taxation's ruling, which effectively abolishes service trusts (the key vehicle via which partnerships protect assets, pay salaries, rent premises etc.), mean that the financial imperatives for the incorporation of law firms have never been greater.[10]

The advent in New South Wales of incorporated legal practices that are increasingly also multidisciplinary practices represents the response of both the profession and the legislature to the changing legal services market. These innovatively structured practices are able to avail themselves of the opportunities and protections afforded by incorporation, and are capable of delivering more streamlined, whole-of-transaction services to clients. They also offer (potentially) greater profit to those who own them.

However, interviews with key informants, including not only regulators but also solicitors and barristers, indicated that they also generate new and more complex forms of ethical problems for the profession and its regulators. Evidently, this is in part due to the increasing pressure for law firms to operate as businesses (as opposed to the traditional view of law as a profession) and to do so in a changing organizational and regulatory environment.

For example, a company's primary duty is to its shareholders, and this is usually interpreted, principally, as an obligation to return maximum profit, as well

---

9 Provision was made elsewhere in Australia prior to 2004 for incorporated legal practices but not incorporated multidisciplinary practices. in Victoria, for instance, the Legal Practice Act 1996 (Vic) required that the sole object of an incorporated legal practice was to engage in legal practice or the practice of foreign law and that all directors be legal practitioners (National Competition Policy Review of the Legal Profession Act 1987, Chapter Ten – The Business Associations of Solicitors and Barristers, available through Lawlink NSW (www.lawlink.nsw.gov.au/report%5Clpd_reports.nsf/pages/ncp_10)).

10 Information provided by Molly Hutcherson, Office of the NSW Legal Services Commissioner.

as to meet disclosure requirements in order that investors may make informed decisions about their investment. However, one of a lawyer's key professional responsibilities is to his or her client, and includes a duty to act in the client's best interests (which may, for example, mean advising a client *not* to pursue legal action) and to maintain strict confidentiality.

Again, what counts as legal work for the purposes of holding accountable an incorporated multidisciplinary practice staffed, on the one hand, by solicitors offering 'legal advice on tax laws' (supposedly within the solicitors' framework of strict professional accountability) and, on the other hand, by tax experts offering 'tax advice in the context of current tax laws' (outside the solicitors' framework)?

If the lines of accountability have become blurred and/or unenforceable, does this mean that ethical responsibilities are now different? It is in recognition of some of these ethical and closely related compliance problems that a measure of institutional redesign has taken place – for example, the introduction of the role of a solicitor-director.

Competition theory, prevalent in all Western countries today, takes economic efficiency as its key goal. This stands in stark contrast to the traditional purpose of the legal profession – the administration of justice, abstracted from concepts of profitability and economic efficiency. This tension between what might be termed the 'profit motive' and the perception that it conflicts with professional ethical practice, is becoming more and more evident in the legal services market today as law firms are increasingly abandoning their traditional structures and choosing to incorporate.

Consequently, the Office of the Legal Services Commissioner (OLSC), as the primary regulator of the legal profession in New South Wales in the context of an overall co-regulatory system – involving also the NSW Law Society and the NSW Bar Association – is reconsidering traditional methods of regulation in favour of new techniques and strategies such as an 'education towards compliance strategy'.

The OLSC approach to regulating these new business structures is much more a 'bottom up' compliance strategy than the prescriptive, 'top down' approaches adopted by other jurisdictions. Rather than prescribing compliance strategies, the OLSC instead requires that compliance systems are developed by the firms themselves. This approach marks a significant shift in the focus of regulation. For the first time in NSW history, the regulatory response now goes beyond addressing individual complaints to effecting cultural change within the profession as a whole, as regulation of the legal services industry moves from regulation of the profession itself to regulation of the provision of legal services.

The reduction of complaints against lawyers is a primary objective of the OLSC. Consequently, the Commissioner is granted a wide range of powers under the *Legal Profession Act 2004*. These powers include, inter alia, the power to suspend or cancel practising certificates and a power of audit of all law firms to ensure compliance with the LPA and associated rules and regulations. In relation to ILPs, this power of audit extends specifically to determining whether a firm has implemented and maintained 'appropriate management systems'.

The LPA requires that ILPs have at least one legal practitioner director who holds an unrestricted practising certificate; the LPA provides for additional responsibilities for legal practitioner directors beyond those responsibilities that partners, sole practitioners and ILP employee solicitors have. The additional responsibilities include:

- the implementation and maintenance of 'appropriate management systems' to enable the provision of legal services in accordance with the professional obligations of solicitors and the other obligations imposed by or under the LPA;[11]
- failure to implement and maintain 'appropriate management systems' is declared to be professional misconduct.[12]

Of course, the legal practitioner director and employed solicitors owe the normal duties in relation to professional obligations, trust funds, legal fees and so on, and members of the ILP who hold practicing certificates are still subject to the provisions of the LPA generally.

The OLSC has worked closely with the Law Society, LawCover (the provider of professional indemnity insurance in New South Wales) and the College of Law (the largest provider of continuing legal education in New South Wales) to develop an educative programme to assist legal practitioner directors to comply with their professional responsibilities.

The OLSC, by agreement with the Law Society, has in practice assumed the role of auditing ILPs for compliance with the LPA and Regulations.

While it is self-evident that the design and implementation of appropriate management systems are at the heart of attempts to deal with ethical and compliance problems within ILPs, the LPA does not define 'appropriate management systems'. Accordingly, the OLSC has collaborated with the Law Society, the College of Law, LawCover, legal practices and other stakeholders to determine the key objectives of an appropriate management system. The approach formulated is an 'education towards compliance' strategy in which ILPs must show that they have procedures in place that show compliance with what the OLSC considers the proper objectives of ethically sound legal practice, including the following:

- competent work practices to avoid negligence;
- timely identification and resolution of the many different incarnations of conflicts of interest, including when acting for both parties to a transaction or acting against previous clients, as well as potential conflicts that may arise in relationships with debt collectors and mercantile agencies or

11 s140(3) of the LPA.

12 The term 'appropriate management systems' is not defined in the LPA.

conducting another business, referral fees and commissions, etc;
- undertakings to be given with authority, monitoring of compliance and timely compliance with notices, orders, rulings, directions or other requirements of regulatory authorities, such as the OLSC, Law Society, courts or costs assessors; and
- avoiding breaches of the LPA in relation to trust accounts.

To enable legal practitioner directors to assess their management systems, a standard 'self-assessment' document has been developed and is sent to all legal practitioner directors as part of the ILP review programme. It is acknowledged that since ILPs vary in terms of size, work practices and nature of operations, an approach of 'one size fits all' requiring the fulfilment of uniform criteria would not be appropriate.

In order to complement the above-mentioned qualitative study of a range of occupations, we undertook a more sustained and focused quantitative study of a single occupational group, namely, solicitors. We selected the solicitors for two main reasons.

- They had a substantial database that we could interrogate with some prospect of extracting substantive results. That said, their database had significant limitations both in terms of the data held, and the form in which it was held; we refer to some of these problems, below.
- Solicitors have a well-developed integrity system – although by no means a complete one.

This study demonstrated the efficacy of the self-assessment system in identifying and monitoring high-complaint firms. The self-assessment instrument is consistent with the ideal of self-regulation, and is a useful quantitative component of an ethical integrity system.

Quantitative Study of Incorporated Legal Practices

The empirical study on *Complaints and Self-Assessment Data Analysis in Relation to Incorporated Legal Practices* (ILPs) was undertaken for the Office of the Legal Services Commissioner (OLSC).[13]

The project involved:

(i) establishing an electronic database derived from (a) data about ILPs; (b) existing complaints data; and (c) self-assessment forms provided by ILPs

13 Miller, S., and Ward, M., *Complaints and Self-Assessment Data Analysis in Relation to Incorporated Legal Practices*, Report for the Office of the Legal Services Commissioner, 2006.

as part of an OLSC self-assessment process for ILPs;
(ii) the development of an instrument to interrogate this database; and
(iii) a quantitative analysis of the database.

The report sets out the findings of this quantitative analysis.

Some Major Findings

- 63% of self-assessment forms (SAFs) were returned with substantial comment thereon.
- 56% of ILPs were prompted to make management system changes by the self-assessment process.
- On 155 occasions some firm or other subsequently reached compliance in relation to one of the ten appropriate management system compliance objectives identified by the OLSC –for instance the objective of timely identification and resolution of conflicts of interest – after initially reporting non-compliance or partial compliance in relation to that commandment.

These findings indicate that the self-assessment process is being taken seriously and is having significant impact.

- Approximately 70% of all complaints were classed as consumer disputes, and 30% of all complaints as investigations and, therefore, classed as more serious matters.
- 75% of all complaints emanated from clients.
- Complaints emanating from practitioners, as opposed to clients, were highly likely to be classed as investigations (67% and 19% respectively).
- A significant percentage (26%) of complaints classed as investigations emanated from the regulator, indicating a proactive approach on the part of the regulator.
- Of the complaints investigated by the OLSC approximately 22% were upheld and of those investigated by the Law Society approximately 79% were upheld. 'Upheld' indicates that the legal practitioner (complainee) was found to have been in some way at fault or was required to remedy the complainant in some way.

These figures are one indicator of the high/low quality of the investigative process. They indicate a reasonably high level of quality in the investigative processes by both the OLSC and the Law Society. Moreover, since most of the investigations conducted by the Law Society are referred from the OLSC, these figures are also one indicator of success/failure in relation to the role of the OLSC in referring matters for investigation to the Law Society. There appears therefore to be a reasonably high level of success of the OLSC in this regard.

Complaints are categorized by the OLSC into categories and sub-categories, for example, Ethical Matters is a category having as one of its sub-categories Misleading or False Advertising.

In relation to the OLSC categorization of complaint categories and sub-categories:

- The generic category of Ethical Matters involved the highest number of complaints (30% of all complaints) followed by Quality of Service (24%) and Costs/bills/agreements (17%).
- The main categories of complaint were subdivided into More Serious and Less Serious. Ethical Matters (More Serious) ranked equal first with Quality of Service (More Serious). That is, each of these two More Serious sub-category types ranked above all the Less Serious sub-category types. Ethical Matters (More Serious) and Quality of Service (More Serious) each contained approximately 22% of all complaint elements (by OLSC sub-category).

Ethical Matters (More Serious) comprises (amongst other complaint types) complaints in relation to conflict of interest, breach of confidentiality, failure to honour undertakings, acting without instructions, misleading or dishonest conduct about progress in court, and misleading advertising. Quality of Service (More Serious) comprises only complaints in relation to negligence and delay.

Among the objects of the data analysis project was comparison of complaints data for ILPs with their reported levels of compliance with the statutory requirement to implement and maintain appropriate management systems as indicated by the ratings ('SAF Ratings') returned by legal practitioner directors on the OLSC Self Assessment Form (SAF) for the ten key management system objectives identified by the OLSC.

Comparing complaint rates for ILPs with reported compliance levels as indicated by the number of Non-Compliant (NC), Partially Compliant (PC), etc., SAF Ratings returned for the ten SAF Objectives yielded various results, including the following. There was a positive correlation between abnormally low reported compliance levels and relatively high complaint rates: there were 46 ILPs who were rated by respondents as being non-compliant or only partially compliant with respect to three or more SAF Objectives and for these 46 ILPs the average number of complaints per solicitor per annum was a relatively high 0.693.

Evidence-based Institutional Design: Designing-in Ethics

Data gathering, aggregation and analysis have been frequently mentioned in the above empirical work. Such data include: (i) aggregated complaints data; (ii) data such as compliance with ethics assurance processes (extracted, for example, from self-assessment exercises); (iii) number of investigations (and percentages of investigated complaints upheld); (iv) data from ethics attitude surveys involving ethical scenarios that elicit the ethical attitudes of practitioners; (v) data from ethics audits (perhaps used in conjunction with reputational indexes); (vi) qualitative data from interviews and focus groups. And there are various other sorts of data sources that can be used. The general point here is that there is no substitute for actual evidence when it comes to the designing and re-designing of integrity systems. Accordingly, the business of developing, maintaining and improving ethico-professional standards should be evidence-based.

Here, there are a number of key questions that need to be addressed, including the following. First, the identification of specific ethical issues confronting particular occupational groups. It is a mistake to think that solicitors' ethical problems are always and everywhere identical with those of engineers or real estate salesmen. Second, a determination needs to be made in relation to the seriousness and frequency of ethical transgressions in a given occupation or professional practice at a given time. Third, specific processes need to be designed and implemented in relation to such problem areas, e.g. conflicts of interest disclosure and avoidance. Fourth, audits need to be conducted to determine that processes are in place and are working. Fifth, the different working parts of the overall integrity system for an occupational group or particular professional practice need to be appropriately integrated. And there are various other important questions that need to be addressed.

However, our first fundamental point is that in relation to all these questions there is a need to investigate, to collect and aggregate data, and to analyse these data. Our second fundamental point is that the results of such evidence-based analysis need to be deployed for the purpose of designing and re-designing integrity systems and the elements thereof. In short, we are recommending evidence-based institutional design and, in particular – given our focus is on ethico-professional standards – the practice referred to in the Introduction to this book as *evidence-based designing-in ethics*.

Bibliography

Accounting Professional and Ethical Standards Board (APESB) 'Compiled APES 110 Code of Ethics for Accountants' (February 2008), at http://www.apesb.org.au/standards.php?id=10 (accessed 14 September 2009).

Adams, G., and Balfour, D., *Unmasking Administrative Evil*, Thousand Oaks: Sage Publications, 1998.

Alexandra, A., and Miller, S., 'Needs, Moral Self-consciousness and Professional Roles', *Professional Ethics*, vol. 5, nos. 1 & 2, 1996, pp. 43–61.

Alexandra, A., and Miller, S., 'Ethical Theory, "Common Morality" and Professional Obligations', *Theoretical Medicine and Bioethics*, vol. 30, no. 1, 2009, pp. 69–80.

Alexandra, A., and Miller, S., *Ethics in Practice: Moral Theory and the Professions*, Sydney: University of NSW Press, 2009.

Alexandra, A., Campbell, T., Cocking, D., Miller, S., and White, K., *Professionalisation, Ethics and Integrity: The Promotion of Professional Ethical Standards and the Protection of Clients and Customers*, Report for the Professional Standards Council, 2006, pp. 1–185.

Aristotle, *The Nichomachean Ethics* (any edition).

Ayres, I., and Braithwaite, J., *Responsive Regulation*, Oxford: Oxford University Press, 1992.

Barker, S., 'What is a Profession?' *Professional Ethics*, vol. 1, nos.1 & 2, 1992, pp. 73–99.

Bayles, M.D., 'Professional Power and Self-Regulation', *Business and Professional Ethics Journal*, vol. 5, no. 2, 1986, pp. 26–43.

Behr, P., and Witt, A., 'Visionary's Dream Led to Risky Business', *Washington Post*, 28 July 2002.

Camenisch, P., 'Business Ethics: On Getting to the Heart of the Matter', *Business and Professional Ethics Journal*, vol. 1, no. 1, 1981, pp. 59–69.

Campbell, T., and Houghton, K. (eds), *Ethics and Auditing*, Canberra: ANU E Press, 2005.

Carr-Saunders, A.M., and Wilson, P.A., *The Professions*, Oxford: Clarendon Press, 1933.

Clarke, F.G., Dean, G.W., and Oliver, K.C., *Corporate Collapse: Regulatory, Accounting and Ethical Failure*, Cambridge: Cambridge University Press, 1998.

Clarke, S., and Oakley, J., 'Informed Consent and Surgeons' Performance', *Journal of Medicine and Philosophy*, vol. 29, no. 1, 2004, pp. 11–35.

Coady, M., and Bloch, S. (eds), *Codes of Ethics and the Professions*, Melbourne: Melbourne University Press, 1996.

Collins, R., 'Market Closure and the Conflict Theory of Professions', in M. Burrage and R. Torstendahl (eds), *Professions in Theory and History*, London: Sage Publications, 1990.

Davies, M., 'Conflict of Interest', *Encyclopedia of Applied Ethics*, Academic Press, 1998, Volume 1.

Davies, M., *Medical Self-regulation*, Aldershot: Ashgate, 2006.

Davis, M., 'Thinking Like an Engineer: The Place of a Code of Ethics in the Practice of a Profession', *Philosophy and Public Affairs*, 20, 1991, pp. 150–167.

Final Report: Learning from Bristol: the report of the public inquiry into children's heart surgery at the Bristol Royal Infirmary 1984-1995, Command Paper: CM 5207 http://www.bristol-inquiry.org.uk/index.htm (accessed 20 June 2009).

Fitzpatrick, M., 'After Bristol: the Humbling of the Medical Profession', *Spiked*, 16 August 2001, at http://www.spiked-online.com/Articles/00000002D1F4.htm (accessed 3 July 2009).

Frais, A., 'Whistleblowing Heroes – Boon or Burden?', *Bulletin of Medical Ethics*, No. 170, August 2001, pp. 13–17.

Friedson, E., 'Nourishing Professionalism', in E.D. Pelligrino, R.M. Veatch and J.P. Langan (eds), *Ethics, Trust and the Professions: Philosophical and Cultural Aspects*, Washington, DC: Georgetown University Press, 1991.

Hibbard, J., Stockard, J., and Tusler, M., 'Hospital Performance Reports: Impact on Quality, Market Share and Reputation', *Health Affairs*, vol. 24, no. 4, 2005, pp. 1150–1160.

Hodson, N., 'Why Auditors Can't Find Fraud', in J. O'Brien (ed.), *Private Equity, Corporate Governance and the Dynamics of Capital Market Regulation*, London: Imperial College of London Press, 2007.

Kant, I., *Groundwork to the Metaphysics of Morals* (any edition).

LaDuke, S., 'The Effects of Professional Discipline on Nurses', *The American Journal of Nursing*, vol. 100, no. 6, June 2000, pp. 26–33.

Lamont, J., 'The Ethics of Doctor Supply Restriction in Australia', *Australian Journal of Professional and Applied Ethics*, vol. 2, no. 2, 2001, pp. 10–19.

Lennane, K.J., '"Whistleblowing": a Health Issue', *British Medical Journal*, 307, 1993, pp. 667–670.

Lichtenberg, J., 'What are Codes of Ethics For?', in M. Coady and S. Bloch (eds), *Codes of Ethics and the Professions*, Melbourne: Melbourne University Press, 1996.

McLeod, R., 'Blowing the Official Whistle', Address by R. McLeod AM, Commonwealth Ombudsman, to *Transparency International Whistleblowing Symposium*, Sydney, August 2002.

Mencimer, S., 'The White Wall. A New Code of Conduct is Taking Hold of the Medical Profession: First Do No Harm—To Your Colleagues', at http://www.

legalaffairs.org/issues/March-April-2004/story_mencimer_marpar04.msp (accessed 17 March 2009).
Mill, J.S., *Utilitarianism* (any edition).
Miller, S., *Social Action: A Teleological Account*, New York: Cambridge University Press, 2001.
Miller, S., *Model Code of Ethics*, Sydney: Professional Standards Council, 2002.
Miller, S., 'Individual Autonomy and Sociality', in F. Schmitt (ed.), *Socialising Metaphysics: Nature of Social Reality*, Lanham: Rowman & Littlefield, 2003, pp. 269–300.
Miller, S., 'Corruption', *Stanford Encylopedia of Philosophy*, Summer edition, 2005.
Miller, S., 'Collective Moral Responsibility: An Individualist Account', in P.A. French (ed.), *Midwest Studies in Philosophy*, vol. XXX, 2006, pp. 176–193.
Miller, S., 'Institutions, Integrity Systems and Market Actors', in J. O'Brien (ed.), *Private Equity, Corporate Governance and the Dynamics of Capital Market Regulation*, London: Imperial College Press, 2007, pp. 297–327.
Miller, S., 'Research in Applied Ethics: Problems and Perspectives', *Philosophia*, vol. 37, no. 2, 2009, pp. 185–201.
Miller, S., *The Moral Foundations of Social Institutions: A Philosophical Study*, New York: Cambridge University Press, 2009.
Miller, S., and Blackler, J., *Ethical Issues in Policing*, Aldershot: Ashgate, 2005.
Miller, S., and Ward, M., *Complaints and Self-Assessment Data Analysis in Relation to Incorporated Legal Practices*, Report for the Office of the Legal Services Commissioner, 2006, pp. 1–45.
Miller, S., Roberts, P., and Spence, E., *Corruption an Anti-Corruption*, Saddle River, NJ: Prentice Hall, 2005.
Murphy, R., *Social Closure: The Theory of Monopolization and Exclusion*, Oxford: Clarendon Press, 1988.
National Competition Policy Review of the Legal Profession Act 1987, Chapter Ten—The Business Associations of Solicitors and Barristers, at www.lawlink.nsw.gov.au/report%5Clpd_reports.nsf/pages/ncp_10.
Newton, L., 'The Origins of Professionalism: Sociological Conclusions and Ethical Implications', *Business and Professional Ethics Journal*, vol. 1, no. 4, 1982, pp. 33–49.
Noonan, J.T., *Bribes*, New York: Macmillan, 1984.
Nye, J., 'Corruption and Political Development', *American Political Science Review*, vol. 61, no. 2, 1967, pp. 417–427.
Organisation for Economic Co-operation and Development (OECD), *Convention Against Bribery of Foreign Public Officials in International Business Transactions*, 15 February 1999.
Peterson, M.J., *The Medical Profession in Mid-Victorian England*, Berkeley: University of California Press, 1978.
Rose-Ackerman, S., *Corruption and Government: Causes, Consequences and Reform*, New York: Cambridge University Press, 1999.

Rothschild, J., and Miethe, T.D., 'Disclosing Misconduct in Work Organizations: An Empirical Analysis of the Situational Factors That Foster Whistleblowing', *Research in the Sociology of Work*, vol. 8, 1999, pp. 211–227.

Rothschild, J., and Miethe, T.D., 'Whistle-Blower Disclosures and Management Retaliation', *Work and Occupations*, vol. 26, no. 1, 1999, pp. 107–128.

Sampford, C., Smith, R., and Brown, A.J., 'From Greek Temple to Bird's Nest: Towards a Theory of Coherence and Mutual Accountability for National Integrity Systems', *Australian Journal of Public Administration*, vol. 64, no. 2, 2005, pp. 96–108.

Savage, D.A., 'The Professions in Theory and History: The Case of Pharmacy', *Business and Economic History*, vol. 23, 1994, pp. 129–160.

Sawyer, K., Johnson, J., and Holub, M. 'The Necessary Illegitimacy of the Whistleblower', at http://papers.ssrn.com/sol3/papers.cfm?abstract_id=917316 (accessed 4 June 2009).

Siggins, I., 'Professional Codes: Some Historical Antecedents', in M. Coady and S. Bloch (eds), *Codes of Ethics and the Professions*, Melbourne: Melbourne University Press, 1996.

Stiglitz, J., *Making Globalization Work: The Next Steps to Global Justice*, London: Penguin, 2006.

Sykes, T., *The Bold Riders*, Sydney: Allen and Unwin, 1994.

Uff, J., *Engineering Ethics: Do Engineers Owe Duties to the Public?*, London: Royal Academy of Engineering, 2002.

Van den Hoven, J., 'Computer Ethics and Moral Methodology', *Metaphilosophy*, vol. 28, no. 3, 1997, pp. 234–249.

Victorian Code of Ethics and Minimum Service Standards for Professional Members of OHS Associations, at http://www.sia.org.au/about/ethics/ (accessed 5 July 2009).

Whittingham, R.B., *Preventing Corporate Accidents: An Ethical Approach*, London: Butterworth-Heinemann, 2008.

Wiggins, D., 'Claims of Need', in D. Wiggins, *Needs, Values, Truth: Essays in the Philosophy of Value*, 2nd edn, Oxford: Blackwell, 1991.

Willis, E., *Medical Dominance*, Sydney: Allen and Unwin, 1990.

World Bank, *Helping Countries Combat Corruption*, Washington, DC: World Bank, 1997.

Index

For Product Safety Concerns and Information please contact our EU representative GPSR@taylorandfrancis.com
Taylor & Francis Verlag GmbH, Kaufingerstraße 24, 80331 München, Germany

www.ingramcontent.com/pod-product-compliance
Ingram Content Group UK Ltd.
Pitfield, Milton Keynes, MK11 3LW, UK
UKHW022122190926
475702UK00013B/1599
* 9 7 8 1 1 3 8 2 7 6 9 2 5 *

Ecological Consequences of Climate Change

Mechanisms, Conservation, and Management